THE
TALENT
EQUATION

THE
TALENT
EQUATION

Big Data Lessons
for Navigating the Skills Gap and
Building a Competitive Workforce

MATT FERGUSON
LORIN HITT
PRASANNA TAMBE
WITH **RYAN HUNT** AND
JENNIFER SULLIVAN GRASZ

New York   Chicago   San Francisco   Athens   London
Madrid   Mexico City   Milan   New Delhi
Singapore   Sydney   Toronto

1 2 3 4 5 6 7 8 9 0   DOC/DOC   1 9 8 7 6 5 4 3

ISBN   978–0–07–182712–6
MHID   0–07–182712–9

e-ISBN   978–0–07–182713–3
e-MHID   0–07–182713–7

Library of Congress Cataloging-in-Publication Data

Ferguson, Matt.
  The talent equation : big data lessons for navigating the skills gap and building a competitive workforce / by Matt Ferguson, CEO of CareerBuilder; Lorin Hitt, University of Pennsylvania, Wharton School; Prasanna Tambe, New York University, Stern School.
    pages cm
  Includes bibliographical references and index.
  ISBN–13:   978–0–07–182712–6 (alk. paper)
  ISBN–10:   0–07–182712–9 (alk. paper)
  1. Manpower planning.   2. Skilled labor.   3. Human capital—Management.
  4. Employees—Recruiting.   5. Employees—Training of.   6. Vocational education.
  I. Hitt, Lorin M. (Lorin Moultrie)   II. Tambe, Prasanna.   III. Title.
  HF5549.5.M3F46 2014
  658.3'01—dc23   2013020474

Contents

Acknowledgments vii

Introduction: Big Data and HR ix

CHAPTER 1: Navigating the Skills Gap and the Shifting
Labor Market 1

CHAPTER 2: An Absolute Good: Education's Value to Workers
and Employers 31

CHAPTER 3: Tenure's Effect on Market Performance 57

CHAPTER 4: Empowering Employment: Training, Reskilling,
and Hiring for Potential 81

CHAPTER 5: A Better Candidate Experience 113

CHAPTER 6: Recruiting in the Digital Era 149

CHAPTER 7: Retaining Talent in Critical Functions 175

CONCLUSION: Investing in the Most Important Asset 207

Notes 211

Index 225

Acknowledgments

Numerous individuals were indispensable in the production of this book. We especially thank the CareerBuilder executives and product managers whose work underlies much of the data and content seen throughout the text, including: Brent Rasmussen, president of CareerBuilder North America; Rosemary Haefner, vice president of human resources; Hope Gurion, chief development officer; Jennifer Seith, managing director of Talent Network; Abdel Tefridji, vice president of workforce analytics; Sanja Licina, senior director of workforce analytics; and Eric Presley, chief technology officer, and Roger Fugett, senior vice president of IT, who along with Dan Cosey and Rob Wittes, were instrumental in implementing CareerBuilder's Re-employment Initiative.

We owe our gratitude to the many talented sales executives and representatives whose work with clients made the interviews for this book possible, including: John Smith, president, Enterprise Sales; Jason Lovelace, president, CareerBuilder Healthcare; Eric Gilpin, president, Staffing and Recruiting Group; as well as, Brian Donahue, William Emmons, Andrew Streiter, Beth Prunier, Jon Ralph, Steve Million, Laura Lynn, Jason Stewart, Brian Johnson, and Matt Laurinas.

We appreciate the support given by the professionals and economists at Economic Modeling Specialists International (EMSI)—CEO Andrew Crapuchettes, Hank Robison, Tim Nadreau, Josh Wright, and Rob Sentz. Additionally, we are grateful for the insightful comments offered by Puneet Manchanda, chair of marketing and professor of marketing at the Ross School of Business at the University of Michigan.

Special thanks are in order to Anthony Balderrama, Debra Auerbach, Susan Ricker, Matt Tarpey, and Amy McDonnell for reviewing the text and lending a wonderful editing eye. For her work organizing the book's many tables and figures, we also thank Susan Moye. We are also grateful for the ideas and support offered by other members of CareerBuilder's marketing team: Jamie Womack, Stephanie Gaspary, Leah Mckelvey, Mike Erwin, Keith Hadley, Mary Lorenz, Justin Thompson, and Jenny Weigle. Finally, we thank CareerBuilder's Ellen Silva, Jonathan Seaver, and Brianna Greene for their help acquiring key information for this project.

Introduction: Big Data and HR

Big data is a big differentiator. Every day, according to IBM, the world creates 2.5 quintillion bytes of data. For the record, quintillion has 18 zeros. IBM contends that 90 percent of the data published today has been created in the last two years alone. Much of that data can be used to make smarter, faster and higher-yielding business decisions.[1]

Large companies are undoubtedly familiar with the applications of big data, but until recently the focus has been primarily on the consumer end. Every click of our mouse and swipe of our credit card leaves behind a trail of data, and companies are racing to collect it, store it, and learn from it. As a result, segmenting consumer behavior first through sales receipts and later through web analytics has revolutionized sales and marketing. It continues to evolve today. The predictive behavior models that the best consumer goods companies use are essentially able to determine what their customers want before they even know they want it. The ability to process and learn from these datasets is as important as the product or service itself to overall market performance.

Seeing this obvious success, executives around the country are now asking: What can big data do for human resources? Think about the massive amount of information a company keeps on their employees—work histories, demographic profiles, education levels, skills competencies, compensation and benefit figures, performance and productivity measures—there's practically no end to the information residing within the typical HR department. As is the case with most data stored on servers or in file cabinets, however, human capital data is widely untouched, due to an inability or lack of initiative to steamline, process, store, and, most importantly, analyze it.

The Talent Equation is about using an incredible quantity of human capital data to create achievable solutions for leaders in the C-suite and HR. Emphasis on this topic was in part refueled by the success of the 2011 film (and 2003 Michael Lewis book of the same name) *Moneyball*, which depicted how the mid-market, payroll-challenged Oakland A's competed with the cash-rich ball clubs by using advanced statistics to gain a recruiting edge. Similarly, attracting, retaining, and maximizing the returns of personnel do not have to be subjective guessing games. Focused data analysis can help companies find, train, and retain the right people in spite of potential skills shortages, resource limitations, and other recruiting challenges:

▶ Predictive analytics on labor supply and demand are helping companies decide where to open new facilities or in which markets they'll find a higher concentration of specialized worker skill sets.

▶ Smart data analysis helps organizations put an end to common screening practices like skipping over job hoppers' resumes or candidates who've been unemployed for a long period of time. Evolv, an HR data research firm, found that new hires in these categories were no more or less likely to be fired or leave voluntarily than other employees. Big data helps applicant-to-employer matching technologies by identifying job titles and skill sets that could lend themselves to similar positions, but are often lost in translation.

▶ Real-time, market-by-market salary and compensation data helps HR leadership keep offers competitive for highly skilled workers in fields like IT or engineering, who often field multiple offers simultaneously.

▶ Candidate experience analysis helps companies rewrite how applicants interface with screening systems, resume software, and company recruiters—a process that can reduce the cost of hire and attract the best talent pool possible.

We'll cover many of these issues and several others throughout the course of this book. However, the potential rewards of this discussion are nullified if talent management executives and other senior leadership don't ask themselves this key question: Is our HR department equipped to flip the big data switch? HR consultant Josh Bersin notes that only 6 percent of HR departments think they are "excellent" at data analytics.[2] But this isn't just an HR problem. Ironically, finding the right talent to tell stories around the data is one of the greatest threats to its utilization. The McKinsey Global Institute predicts that in just six years the U.S. will be short up to 1.5 million data analysts and business managers capable of putting the complex data at their fingertips to use.[3] The economic cost of the potential inefficiencies is truly astounding.

This is a good reminder that the potential of big data carries with it a warning. There's an inherent risk in assuming all data is relevant data or that all data is truth. In reality, the bigger the data gets, the more difficult reigning it in becomes. It takes a careful eye to parse meaningful correlations from alluring, but ultimately misleading, results. Just as there are consequences for relying too heavily on nonempirical, "going from the gut" decision making, data analytics must be a measured, scientific endeavor.

There's one more important, persuasive benefit to the careful use of data analysis: It provides a gateway for HR to gain even more leverage within the C-suite. The more HR provides metrics about the efficacy of current strategies or the potential benefits of new strategies, the more the C-suite will see them as indispensable business partners. Human capital is almost always an organization's primary investment. Knowing that, it makes sense that empirical, data-backed recommendations for getting the most from that investment will have more success at getting the attention of senior leaders. HR departments are being cut back at a time when attracting and developing the right talent is often the key marketplace differentiator among firms. With the right tools and information, HR professionals can reverse this trend.

This book is designed to highlight the potential of big data in HR and showcase several examples that are a living testament to that potential. We'll analyze data from public and private sectors, information from more than 50 million resumes, and hundreds of thousands of survey responses. Throughout, we'll sit down with recruiters and human resources leadership at major American companies—each, of course, is out to hire the best minds. From workforce education levels to the effects of candidate experience on recruitment strategy, here's a look at the big questions we'll answer.

Chapter 1—Navigating the Skills Gap and the Shifting Labor Market

▶ **How has the labor market changed over recent decades, specifically in the aftermath of the recession?** In recent years, a lack of demand for labor, combined with the threat of a skilled labor shortage, has created an intensely competitive talent market for job seekers and employers alike. We'll discuss the growing debate around the "skills gap"—how talent managers define it, how compensation and lack of training or education play a factor, and ways to mitigate the short-term effects of job vacancies for skilled positions.

▶ **What's the future of the U.S. labor market?** The path to better paying jobs and more opportunities for workers of all skill levels can be found in a national effort to create more knowledge and innovation jobs.

CHAPTER 2—AN ABSOLUTE GOOD: EDUCATION'S VALUE TO WORKERS AND EMPLOYERS

▶ **How does the education level of workers in core functions affect a business's market performance?** Businesses, by default, have made the pursuit of higher education a prerequisite for attaining many high paying jobs in America. You only have to look at the unemployment rates of college-educated workers and high school-educated workers to see the gap in opportunity between these groups. In this chapter, we share new research suggesting a link between a company's market performance and its education levels for certain business functions.

▶ **What are the short- and long-term salary returns of a bachelor's degree or master's degree for workers in specific fields?** As the costs of higher education continue to rise, we explore whether or not it remains a wise investment for most workers.

CHAPTER 3—TENURE'S EFFECT ON MARKET PERFORMANCE

▶ **How do tenure of sales, customer service, information technology, and other functions affect a business's market value? Is there an advantage to having higher retention levels for some functions and lower retention for others?** For some business functions, longer workforce tenure may be beneficial to market performance, but the opposite is true in other areas. Conclusions from the data may prompt executives to analyze tenure and turnover at their organizations, and question where and why long-term experience is a boon or a drag.

Chapter 4—Empowering Employment: Training, Reskilling, and Hiring for Potential

▸ **Is it more beneficial to wait for the right hire, or train workers who are mostly qualified for the job?** If the U.S. economy is to overcome its structural employment challenges, businesses will have to play a role in training necessary workers. Here we'll take a look at companies who, rather than wait for the perfect hire, create the perfect hire.

Chapter 5—A Better Candidate Experience

▸ **Are there bottom-line consequences for a poorly designed job listing and a negative candidate experience during the hiring process?** Based on CareerBuilder's research and survey of more than 5 million job seekers, we explore which factors are most critical to workers in evaluating potential employers, as well as how disappointed job seekers' actions can have an adverse impact on companies.

Chapter 6—Recruiting in the Digital Era

▸ **How have recent changes in the human capital technology market enhanced the recruitment process?** The average job seeker is using up to 15 resources to find a job. Employers, therefore, must rely on a multi-faceted approach to find needed talent. In this chapter, we explore research on continuous recruitment and labor supply and demand tools, as well as the necessity of enhancing mobile recruitment platforms.

CHAPTER 7—RETAINING TALENT IN CRITICAL FUNCTIONS

▶ **What compels a worker to stay loyal to a company and how are companies rebuilding their employment brands to boost retention?** As the labor market improves, it's not uncommon to see a concurrent rise in voluntary turnover. Here we explore data that indicates how leading companies retain core talent.

We hope these questions and the data underlying our conclusions compel you to place your own organization's short- and long-term recruiting strategies under the microscope. It may be a little too optimistic of us to assume all readers will be thrilled to immerse themselves in data and human capital. To some, the two subjects may seem incongruent. Won't big data take the "human" out of human resources? Won't it replace the face-to-face conversations necessary to truly know if a job candidate is the right fit for the business?

We don't see it that way at all.

If anything, the insights learned from the research compiled here provide an easier way to get what we all want: placing the right people in front of the right employers, at the right time.

THE
TALENT
EQUATION

CHAPTER 1

Navigating the Skills Gap and the Shifting Labor Market

Since the official beginning of the economic recovery (June 2009), the labor market has been like a freeway traffic jam: four of the five lanes are stalled completely, or are at best inching forward at a slow crawl. Drivers in these lanes make up most of the job-seeking population. They are former public sector employees—teachers, police officers, city administrators, etc. They are service, retail, construction, and manufacturing workers. They are small business owners who had to shut their doors when credit dried up and business slowed. They are recent graduates competing for finite opportunities and mature workers nearing—but not quite able to reach—retirement. Some drivers have pulled off the freeway altogether, temporarily or permanently quitting their job searches. In fact, the labor force participation rate recently hit a thirty-year low.[1]

This backup is particularly frustrating because there's a sense the unemployment rate should be dropping more quickly. More lanes should be clearing. While still low by historical standards, demand for labor has increased significantly post-recession. The Bureau of Labor Statistics (BLS) counts the number of open jobs at the end of every month. In late 2012, there were anywhere between 3.5 and 3.7 million openings—up from 2.2 million in the summer of 2009. This should be welcome news. More opportunities lead to more unemployed workers heading back to work. Higher demand intuitively leads us to believe the economy is heating up.

However, many job seekers are still left idling. The pace of hiring—now four years after the end of the recession—remains too slow for a vibrant jobs recovery. In early 2013, unemployment remained too high given the demand for labor at the time. If this economic downturn followed similar historical patterns, the unemployment rate should be somewhere between 5.5 and 6 percent. This chapter explores why this is the case and what it means for recruiting and human resources (HR). As we'll see in the coming pages, severe implications exist for both organizations and the economy when the labor market is simultaneously faced with millions of job vacancies and persistently high unemployment. In this discussion, we'll track present and projected shifts in the labor market, as well as what employers can do to attract high-level talent in spite of a competitive recruiting landscape.

There are a number of theories seeking to explain the apparent anomaly between labor demand and job creation. Many hiring managers are taking longer to fill positions. They are under pressure to find the perfect hire and are willing to wait for the person with the right skills mix. Also, it's possible that the housing market crisis created a geographical imbalance between unemployed workers and available positions. Relocation may have become more difficult with so many underwater homeowners. Some labor experts contend that wages offered aren't good enough to attract workers who may have had a much higher paying position before the recession and are willing to stay on unemployment benefits rather than take a severe salary cut. There's likely a bit of truth to all of these ideas. However, there's one more explanation that's received a lot of attention in the press as of late: a structural mismatch between the skills employers need and the skills unemployed job seekers possess—commonly referred to as the skills gap.

The skills gap is a complex issue. While economists are often skeptical of the argument that skill shortages are behind slow job growth, business leaders and hiring managers consistently say they're confronted with a deficit of high-level talent. A 2012 nationwide survey of more than

2,000 HR managers and hiring managers conducted by CareerBuilder and Harris Interactive found that nearly four in ten employers had open positions for which they could not find qualified candidates. Eight in ten employers cited they were concerned by an "emerging skills gap."[2] Based on this data, and countless news reports and anecdotal stories of hiring managers and executives stating they can't find the right talent, it seems to us the skills gap narrative is the most popular explanation for the hiring traffic jam among talent acquisition professionals.

On the ground level, the explanation seems to make sense. Even in the most frustrating jams there seems to be one outside lane that moves a little faster than the rest. Some of these drivers are workers from other lanes merging into new industries or are fortunate enough to find new work, but the majority possess niche skill sets or are highly educated, seizing on the immediate demands of the recovering economy. These include medical professionals, technology workers, engineers, finance and accounting experts, and business development professionals. Many of the best jobs to emerge in the recovery favor science, technology, engineering and math (STEM) skill sets, potentially placing those without these skills in the other lanes of traffic at a disadvantage. Opportunities for some high-skill jobs are growing quickly, while demand for many middle-skill roles lag behind, and in some cases may never come back. Even jobs in the skilled trades are threatened by skills gaps as their predominantly older workforce nears retirement.

The human cost of this situation is summed up by millions of eager and available workers who could be working, but aren't. The job market condition appears to be affecting the long-term unemployed the most. As of December 2012, the share of unemployed workers who've been searching for 27 weeks (about seven months) or more was 40 percent—representing nearly five million people, according to the BLS. This is troublesome because the longer workers remain inactive, the greater the odds normal cyclical unemployment will become structural. Recent college grads aren't able to put new knowledge to work in their field of study. Laid off experienced workers often retire earlier than planned. Discouraged workers stop looking for jobs, and in turn, aren't counted in the unemployment figures despite a desire (and personal need) to contribute to the economy. For all of these workers, skills atrophy over time, making it more difficult to get back in the game.

But suggesting there's a skills gap is not to say unemployed workers are without skills. Nor is it to say the workforce is incapable of competing at a global level, or even that the skills gap is the biggest factor holding back the labor market. Eventually demand for labor will increase and all lanes of hiring will speed up. Saying there's a skills gap or a skills shortage is simply acknowledging that businesses sense a growing imbalance between the supply and demand of highly skilled or specialized labor for certain occupations.

However, conversations about the skills gap shouldn't be married to the present-day labor market. Reconfiguring the skills and education mix is essentially the story of what the labor market will need to do in order to remain competitive and innovative in the coming decades. The longer the economic slump continues, the more we know that this recession was different. More and more economists and business leaders are making this message very public. Economist and scholar Jeffery Sachs, looking at recent trends, concluded in the *Financial Times*:

> "In short, we need new economic strategies to overhaul broken systems of finance, labour markets, taxation, ecological management, budget management and investment incentives … The new approaches must be long-term, structural, sensitive to inequalities of skills and education, aligned with the need for more sustainable technologies and 'smarter' infrastructure (empowered by information technology) and congruent with long-term demographic trends."[3]

The cost of job vacancies to a company stems largely from lost productivity and lost revenue. The cost to the economy is measured in slower growth and fewer opportunities. For these reasons, any mismatch—no matter the cause—should be met proactively. If you're in a position related to talent acquisition, whether that's your full-time job or you occasionally need to hire a new worker to your team, it's important to know that the talent mismatch is a human capital challenge that can be largely addressed through careful planning and honest evaluation of the workforce. In this chapter we discuss how mismatches between the job seeker and the employer can be averted:

▶ First, we'll briefly explore how the labor market has shifted over the last four decades, and how this shift indicates where it's headed in the future.

▶ Second, we'll identify where skills gaps exist according to recruiters and HR managers, and what they see as potential causes.

▶ Third, we'll discuss how companies can use data-driven solutions to fill vacancies more efficiently and avoid mismatches.

▶ Finally, we'll discuss the potential positive economic impact of job creation in high-skill areas.

THE LABOR MARKET—PAST, PRESENT, AND FUTURE

The diversity of the U.S. economy and the breadth of opportunity it affords its citizens is one of the pillars of the nation's success. But changes to the global economy (and the changes wrought by the recession) threaten the idea that one's children should always be left in a better place. If we follow the story of where new jobs are likely to be created, however, a path forward emerges that has stood the test of time: the acquisition of skills and education for a greater share of the workforce.

The potential for this to succeed, in part, hinges on the realization that technology and globalization are changing the composition of the U.S. workforce to a great extent, and are consequently shifting the skills required by the contemporary economy. The work we do now is markedly different than the work we did 40 years ago, and the work we'll do in 10 years will be markedly different than the work we do today. As shown in Figure 1.1, the picture of where Americans work, then and now, tells this story.[4]

What can we take from the shifts represented in Figure 1.1? First, it's clear that the most noticeable change occurred in manufacturing. The share of jobs there has dropped precipitously since 1972—from 24 percent of all jobs to about 9 percent today. There are six million fewer Americans working in the sector than 40 years ago; however, manufacturing remains vital to America's global competitiveness. In terms of pure output, the U.S. remains the global leader, neck and neck with China, but technological advances have decreased the demand for labor at individual firms.

The decline in manufacturing jobs over the last four decades was offset by major growth in private education and health care (20 million jobs in 2012 from 5 million in 1972), business services (18 million jobs in 2012 from 6 million in 1972) and leisure and hospitality (14 million jobs in 2012 from 5 million in 1972). The employment shift represents a steady movement away from the tradable goods sector toward a workforce dominated by the service sector.

But Figure 1.1 is merely a snapshot of two very different points in U.S. economic history. What it doesn't tell us is how the recession changed the landscape of the U.S. labor market. For instance, the percentage of jobs in construction is now below 1972 levels, but this is most certainly a result of the national housing bust and budget crises at the state level. There are two million fewer construction jobs available today than in late 2007—the official start of the recession. When the housing market begins its inevitable turnaround (and there are signs that it's

FIGURE 1.1 | SHARE OF U.S. JOBS BY INDUSTRY: 2012 VS. 1972

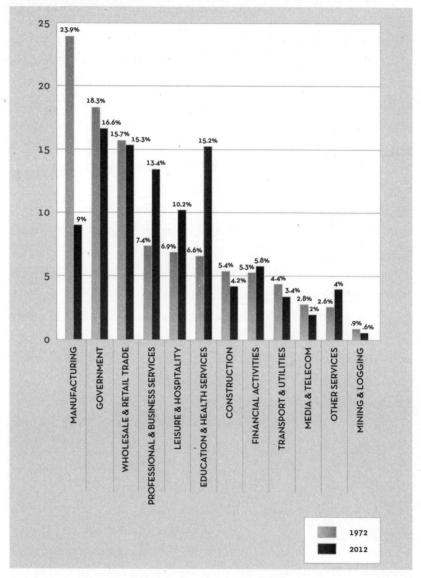

Source: National Public Radio via Bureau of Labor Statistics, 2012

already underway), many of these jobs and other jobs in the supply chain will come back, giving a much needed jolt to the economy. Berkshire Hathaway Chairman and CEO Warren Buffett voiced confidence about the prospects of a housing recovery. In 2012, he announced plans for a nationwide real estate chain that will open 1,700 offices. "People say construction is only four percent of the labor force, but it extends way beyond that," he said in an interview with Fox Business in early 2013, noting that industries ranging from paint to masonry and flooring will benefit. "Those are not construction workers but they [represent] activity in fields that feed off construction. I think that construction coming back is a very important force in the economy." [5]

And yet the story of the recession also tells us that the economy is growing most quickly in industries that increasingly require a larger share of high-knowledge, high-skill workers. Figure 1.2 shows average monthly job creation numbers in the years preceding the recession compared to the years during and after the recession for the major sectors listed.

There are a number of intriguing stories embedded in this graph. For one, we can see how the basic tenets of supply and demand operate in recession-era economies. The restaurant, travel, and retail sectors took a significant dip in the 18-month recession. As consumers rein in expenses, businesses have been forced to adjust the size of their labor pools accordingly. Leisure and hospitality has made up losses incurred in this period, but retail continues to struggle in spite of small gains. The shift toward e-commerce is a likely culprit, as consumers continue spending more of their dollars online year-over-year. On a different path, government employment started declining just as the private sector began heading in a positive direction, primarily because the state aid provisions in the stimulus bill delayed or eliminated the probable layoffs of millions of public sector workers—primarily in education and law enforcement. Unlike the federal government, which can sustain large deficits for longer periods of time, most states' constitutions require that their governors pass balanced budgets, which meant severe cuts when stimulus funds ran dry.

FIGURE 1.2 | JOB GROWTH BY SECTOR: BEFORE, DURING, AND AFTER THE RECESSION

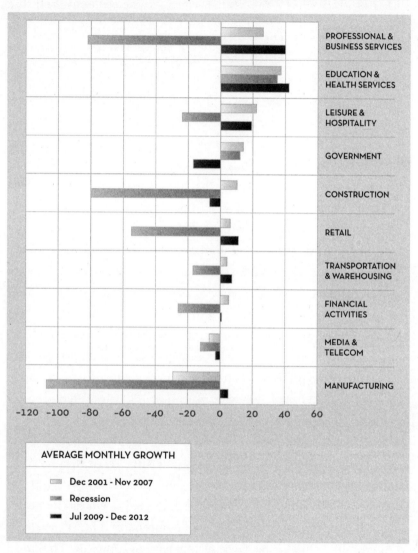

Source: Bureau of Labor Statistics, Establishment Data, 2013

Movement in a few sectors—professional and business services, education, health services, and manufacturing—gives us a significant clue as to where the labor market is headed. For that reason, each needs to be called out in more detail.

The Endurance of Health Care and Private Education

Compared to other major sectors, job creation in private education and health care is a pure outlier. These segments were adding jobs quickly before the recession, they were the only private sector areas to add jobs during the recession, and they continue to add about 13,000 jobs per month. At a time when labor opportunities in every other industry and sector were faltering, education and health services endured, placing themselves on the mantle as truly "recession proof." We first saw evidence of these sectors' durability during the 2001 recession, when education and health services added 50,000 jobs per month. There are a few big reasons for this continued growth. First, demand for health care employment exists outside the lines of normal cyclical economic fluctuations. The demand for medical professionals and health care support positions, especially as the U.S. population ages, won't be as elastic as the demand in other sectors simply because health care decisions take priority over consumption of other goods and services. Meanwhile, private education, including online universities, weathered the most recent recession because many laid off workers often took unemployment as an opportunity to retrain and reskill. Likewise, many new graduates deferred entering a weak labor market, instead choosing graduate school.

But a key reason health care and education services hold a larger share of overall jobs is that, unlike many goods and services, every community needs them. "About half of the jobs created between 1990 and 2008 (before our current downturn) were created in education, health care, and government," wrote Derek Thompson of TheAtlantic.com in August 2012. "What do those sectors have in common? They're all local."[6] In short: They can't be offshored or consolidated in other areas of the country. Globalization hasn't yet changed the demand trajectories for these key segments of our economy because every local economy needs nurses, doctors, child care workers, and educators. Low-skill labor in retail and hospitality can also be grouped this way. An important caveat to this is that there's no guarantee the locality of these jobs will remain permanent. As video, broadband networking, and other web technologies evolve, it's easy to envision labor in many support or administrative functions being replaced by non-local workers in the coming decades in certain areas of education, health care, and retail.

In order to sustain robust economic growth, U.S. businesses must continue to deliver innovative, valuable goods and services. Our value to the world economy will be closely tied to what we give to the world economy. The post-recession data shows that growth is also possible in areas of manufacturing and business services.

THE MANUFACTURING SURGE

Between 2000 and the end of the 2007 recession, the U.S. lost approximately 5.5 million manufacturing jobs. The culprits are largely the forces of globalization and automation. But to the surprise of many economists, a positive trend started in late 2011 and early 2012: Manufacturing went through its first period of sustained job growth since the 1990s. The sector has added 265,000 jobs post-recession. And although it barely made a dent compared to the loss column, economists saw this as welcome news. After a half century of offshoring factory labor, the cost curve is bending back in the favor of the U.S. Moreover, technological innovation such as 3D printing of product prototypes allows small firms to go to market more quickly, which increases the incentive to stay in North America. James Fallows of the *The Atlantic* magazine wrote that such developments could foretell a "renaissance" of manufacturing startups in the U.S.

> "…the latest wave of technological innovation, communications systems, and production tools may now make it easier—especially to bring new products to market faster than the competition by designing, refining, and making them in the United States. At just the same time, social and economic changes in China are making the outsourcing business ever costlier and trickier for all but the most experienced firms."[7]

Despite the positive outlook, few experts expect a return to previous employment levels in U.S. manufacturing, barring a massive expansion of existing firms and the number of new businesses. The fact is, the latest manufacturing resurgence is very different than prior growth periods. American manufacturing is relying less on the quantity of labor and more on the quality and efficiency of its technological capital. Jobs will be fewer, but the skills and knowledge levels required to perform them will be more complex. Machine workers now need to be familiar with engineering and computing principles to successfully operate equipment and fix machinery when it breaks down.

Thus, the future of manufacturing growth in America will likely consist of a surge of many smaller firms that employ a relatively small number of skilled workers. For example, Fallows reported that there are 400 manufacturing firms in San Francisco that make up the coalition SFMade, which draws upon the Bay Area's highly skilled labor pool. Together these firms only employ about 3,000 people. While the number suggests the labor-intensive, high-headcount manufacturing days are receding, there is a silver lining. Because these jobs are for the most part very high paying, they end up supporting other good jobs up and down the supply chain, as well as other service jobs locally.

THE CATAPULT OF PROFESSIONAL AND BUSINESS SERVICES

At the time of this writing, companies in professional and business services have recouped jobs lost during the recession. The wide umbrella in this sector includes IT firms, staffing firms, engineering services, B2B companies, facilities operations, accounting firms, payroll companies, legal services, PR/marketing/advertising agencies, and a host of consulting services. Together, this group is adding more than 40,000 new jobs a month to the economy, a sign that companies in all sectors are gearing up for economic revival.

One in eight jobs created post-recession within business services is in computer systems design or other IT jobs, which makes sense, given the rapid evolution of networking technologies that allow companies to eliminate waste, make decisions faster, and manage their services more efficiently. No company wants to be left behind in the tech race for fear their competitors may lap them on the track. This is why IT is consistently among the top areas HR managers say they're hiring for post-recession. In CareerBuilder's 2012 Annual Job Forecast, 22 percent of HR managers said they planned to hire tech workers before anyone else.

BLS data also shows that nearly half of professional and business services jobs come from the staffing and employment resources industry. While the rapid growth of "temp jobs" suggests firms are still hesitant to take on full headcount in an uncertain, low-demand economy, many staffing jobs transition to permanent roles within companies that pay highly competitive wages. Better yet, despite a common misperception to the contrary, temporary or contract jobs are not solely administrative or clerical positions. They are often in fields such as IT, design, or marketing.

Companies are also investing heavily in customer service and sales positions—a sign that firms are focused again on revenue-driving and functional, rather than cost saving, areas. Sales job listings on CareerBuilder.com grew 17 percent from 2010 to 2011 and 7 percent from 2011 to 2012. Customer service jobs posted similar gains: 27 percent growth in 2011 and 13 percent growth in 2012.

The Future Workforce: Which Jobs and Skills Will Be In Demand?

The McKinsey Global Institute reported in 2012 that by the end of the decade, 36 percent of all jobs in the U.S. will require college-educated workers, compared to 24 percent at the time of the report's publication.

The deficit of college-educated workers will be 1.5 million, should current graduation rates remain stable, and that appears to be a conservative view.[8] Anthony Carnevale of Georgetown University predicted that 63 percent of all occupations will require at least some postsecondary training by 2018.[9] In order to fill that need, the private sector and government must begin collaborating on solutions immediately. The potential lack of supply of high-skill workers will be met at the other end by a major oversupply of low- or medium-skill workers. Globally, across advanced economies, MGI projects a possible 35 million more workers without postsecondary education than companies will actually need.

The BLS biannual employment projections report confirms the threat of a skills or education gap. Employment in the U.S. is projected to grow by more than 14 percent in this decade, and growth of high-skill jobs will outpace the creation of low- or medium-skill positions: "Occupations classified as needing a master's degree are projected to grow by 21.7 percent, followed by doctoral or professional degree occupations at 19.9 percent, and associate degree occupations at 18 percent."[10]

In fact, 17 of the 30 occupations with the fastest projected employment growth this decade require a college degree. Much of the demand will be for workers with STEM degrees. Moreover, three of the occupations on the list that just require a high school diploma are skilled trade positions (stonemasons, brick masons, rebar/iron workers) that can require lengthy apprenticeships. Of these high-growth occupations, here are the top ten that require a college degree and the expected employment growth percentage for each:

1. Biomedical engineers (62 percent)

2. Veterinary technologists (52 percent)

3. Physical therapist assistants (46 percent)

4. Meeting/event planners (44 percent)

5. Diagnostic medical stenographers (44 percent)

6. Occupational therapy assistants (43 percent)

7. Interpreters/translators (42 percent)

8. Market research analysts/marketing specialists (41 percent)

9. Marriage and family therapists (41 percent)

10. Physical therapists (39 percent)

From 2010–2020, the economy will add nearly 250,000 architecture and engineering jobs, 600,000 management jobs, 800,000 jobs in math and computer occupations, more than one million jobs in business and financial occupations, and about two million doctors, nurses, and other technical health care practitioners. This amounts to about five million new jobs in areas that typically require skilled, educated workers. To put it clearly: the number of high-skill or high-education jobs that we'll need to fill by 2020 is roughly equivalent to the populations of Chicago and Houston combined. Even then, those are merely projections of the course we're on currently. A hypothetical influx of additional STEM workers could lead to more new businesses and higher levels of job creation.

Observers of monthly job creation data point out that many of the jobs created post-recession were at the low end of the wage scale. While that may be true, low-skill labor as a share of total employment will gradually decline due to the rise of automation. The BLS report found that twenty-seven of the thirty occupations that expect the largest employment declines do not require postsecondary education. Carnevale summed this up succinctly:

"Occupations with high levels of non-repetitive tasks, such as professional and managerial jobs, tend to require postsecondary education and training. These types of jobs are growing, while positions dominated by repetitive tasks that tend to require high school or less, like production jobs, are declining."

THE KILLER APP: MERGING THE TECHNICAL AND STRATEGIC WORKER

Economic Modeling Specialists International (EMSI), an economic analysis firm specializing in complex labor market data, and Career-Builder released a list of the best bachelor's degree jobs in 2013 based on growth patterns since 2010. The occupations included software developers, accountants, market research analysts, computer systems analysts, mechanical engineers, and financial analysts. For the most part, every job on the list requires proficiency in technical skills. However, a closer look at the job descriptions reveals that employers are primarily in need of individuals who can apply technical expertise in a strategic context. The technical mind is often only as valuable as the person's analytical prowess; critical thinking, problem solving, and communications skills are crucial to an organization's optimization of technical functions. It's not enough to hire hard skills, which is why we see more managers who value technical workers with backgrounds in the liberal arts and humanities—classic areas of higher education that groom dynamic, balanced thinkers capable of wearing many hats within organizations.

The tech world refers to any indispensable computer program or software platform as a "killer app." We believe that the worker who can successfully merge right and left brain skills—the social/strategic with the technical—is the "killer app" of the modern, knowledge-driven labor market. The jobs that are unlikely to ever be offshored or replaced via automation involve what economists call tacit interactions. These are not repetitive transaction jobs, but roles that require the worker to make frequent, complex, context-sensitive decisions. Research conducted using CareerBuilder's extensive resume database leads us to believe that these types of jobs will capture an increasing share of the labor market in the knowledge economy.

In a paper published in *Management Science*, we explored how offshoring in the IT sector is affecting the skills composition of tech workers in the U.S., finding firms that offshore IT services are readjusting their domestic workforce toward occupations requiring greater personal interaction.[11] These jobs include project managers and IT sales, but also hands-on roles, like network administrators, that require a physical presence. We looked at detailed resume information from more than 92,000 U.S.-based IT workers and 64,000 overseas IT workers employed by about 7,500 different firms. After classifying whether or not a job was "tradable" (IT roles that could be feasibly performed anywhere) and controlling for a number of other factors, we found that the percentage of IT workers in tradable jobs has dropped by 8 percentage points at firms that have offshore staff. This has very real implications for U.S.-based IT workers. Namely, technology professionals may find it beneficial to focus on soft skills— such as advanced communication skills or business management—in addition to their mastery of a technical niche.

Company executives often cite that their best workers are not merely efficient producers, but dynamic thinkers, as well. This is not just true of IT, engineering, finance, or other roles that require hard skills. For instance, an effective sales and customer service team is made up of individuals (driven by the same goals) using their personal strengths to meet the diverse needs of the client or customer. It's difficult for a company to write a procedure manual when there are many potential right answers. The Apples, Zappos, and Amazons of the world understand this point well.

Some may argue that the ability to successfully perform these tasks is a product of personality—the skills you can't teach, so to speak. To an extent that may be true, but we'd argue that highly educated workers who've studied a mix of disciplines in college—from computer science and finance to the liberal arts and humanities—are the most likely to have the skills mix necessary to compete and innovate in a knowledge economy.

In the next chapter, we'll discuss just how critical education levels in specific functions are to market performance.

UNDERSTANDING THE TALENT MISMATCH

Now that we have a better idea of how the U.S. labor situation has changed over the past several decades, and where it's very likely headed, let's move on to the next major topics of the chapter: answering where and why mismatches exist.

The skills gap has been at the center of this debate in the press. Every week there's a new story about a company that struggles with an apparent talent mismatch. These employers span industries, and include everything from home-grown small businesses to major corporations.

- ▸ Writing about the rapid growth of tech jobs, Brad Smith, an executive at Microsoft, wrote in the *Wall Street Journal* in 2012 that his company has 3,400 new positions for engineers, researchers, and developers, a 34 percent increase from the year before. The trouble is, according to Smith, about 120,000 new jobs in computer science are created per year, but only 40,000 bachelor's degrees are issued in computer science annually.[12]

- ▸ Many small companies operating under tight budgets struggle to find people with niche skill sets. An owner of a small security firm in Florida has had two technician jobs open for eighteen months. "We could grow a lot faster if we could find the right people," he said.[13] Sweet Water Sound, a professional audio gear internet retailer in Fort Wayne, Indiana, states that even if they get someone with the right technical skills, his or her communication, writing, and sales abilities typically are far behind expectations for the client-centered company. The skills mix is askew. For them, it's better to wait for the right candidate than take a risk.[14]

- ▸ Citing a decline in vocational training programs, the American Welding Society states there's a projected shortage of more than 230,000 welders through 2019. As skilled welders retire, the concern is that not enough younger workers are entering the trade. [15]

Let's recap what's happening in these examples. STEM-related jobs in IT are exploding at a rate that makes it very difficult for some firms to attract necessary talent from a limited labor pool. Smaller companies often don't have the recruiting resources or training budgets to find and acquire skilled workers. On the other hand, some companies would rather be highly selective than take a chance on a worker who doesn't "have all the software" to perform well at the outset of his or her tenure. And finally, a decline in vocational training appears to even be affecting employers offering good-paying blue-collar jobs.

It's easy to point fingers in this situation. Schools may want to blame employers for not collaborating on curricula; companies may want to blame schools for not delivering workers with applicable skill sets; job seekers may want to blame companies for not investing in training or for being too picky. But none of that gets us too far. The reality remains: employers say they have a need to fill vacant positions, and each additional week or month vacancies go unfilled it exacts a very real cost on the economy. With that in mind, let's take a closer look at what employers are saying about vacancies and the skills gap, as well as what we know about the supply and demand of skilled labor. From there, we'll offer a few solutions (some of them big data solutions) that will help employers large and small navigate the skills gap.

A Closer Look at Vacancies

We mentioned at the outset of the chapter that nearly four in ten employers have open positions for which they could not find qualified candidates—48 percent of large businesses, 43 percent of middle market employers, and 36 percent of small businesses (see Table 1.1). Nine out of ten of these jobs are full-time, permanent positions. Unsurprisingly,

TABLE 1.1 | HARDEST POSITIONS TO RECRUIT

Function	Have a hard time filling open positions
Engineering	61%
C-Level	58%
Business Development	57%
Creative/Design	54%
Management Level	48%
Information Technology	47%
Accounting/Finance	44%

Source: CareerBuilder Talent Crunch Study, Harris Interactive, 2012

the job types most affected by this challenge are in areas that require highly educated, specialized, or skilled workers.

For large companies, the survey referenced in Table 1.1 found that IT is the second hardest position to fill behind engineering. To be fair, even in healthy economic times, hiring managers have expressed the wish for a more talented labor pool, but never to this extent. Many of the open jobs hiring managers refer to require skills in new technologies that have no established internal training programs for new hires to attend. In some cases, companies have eliminated their training departments altogether. The survey found that a lack of technical skills is a primary roadblock to hiring candidates, but few companies actually invest in training of these skills.

Another possible explanation for the rise of unfilled positions is that more employers are reporting that their companies have created new job functions that didn't exist at their organizations five years ago. About one in ten companies have new positions in financial regulation, diversity, green energy and the environment, and global relations. New tech positions also continue to dominate emerging jobs: 12 percent of companies have new positions in cybersecurity, 15 percent have new positions in data storage and management, and 16 percent have positions tied to social media.

In some cases, hiring managers prefer that their new engineers, developers, and candidates for other skilled positions are ready immediately upon hire. But as we'll see, there can be a very real, very high cost to leaving positions open for too long.

WHERE IS COMPENSATION INCREASING?

Skeptics of the skills gap's existence point out that we should see high demand for specialized labor reflected in salary. This is a basic economic principle. If the labor market is truly pinched for skilled talent, the workers who are lucky enough to have the in-demand skills should get a significant wage bump. When we look at broad industry sectors, it's hard to see this show up. But dig into specific occupations and job functions, and the evidence is there.

For example, CareerBuilder's 2013 Annual Job Forecast, which surveyed more than 6,000 workers and nearly 3,000 hiring managers, found that IT workers are expected to see the second highest salary increases at their organizations, right behind sales professionals. Three out of ten IT hiring managers planned raises of at least 4 percent—7 percentage points higher than the national average across all sectors and 9 percentage points higher than planned salary increases in 2012. While most workers were expecting base pay to increase between 1 and 3 percent in 2013, high-demand tech occupations often saw raises that ran much higher, as shown in Table 1.2.[16]

But here's where the wage jumps really kick in: According to staffing firm Robert Half International, developers who also have skills in programming languages like C++, Java EE, .NET, and PHP saw an additional 7 to 9 percent added on top of their planned 2013 salaries.

TABLE 1.2 | GROWTH IN SALARY FOR IT DEVELOPERS

Job Title	2012	2013	% Change
Applications Architect	$97,500 - $132,000	$103,750 - $140,500	6.4%
CRM Technical Developer	$80,000 - $106,750	$84,00-$112,250	5.1%
Developer/Program Analyst	$60,750 - $107,500	$64,750-$144,500	6.5%
Mobile Applications Developer	$85,000 - $122,500	$92,750 - $133,500	9%

Source: Robert Half International Salary Guides

Higher wages are not just for high-tech or white-collar jobs. The skills gap and increased pay show up in traditional blue-collar occupations, as well. *The Wall Street Journal* reported in 2011 that wages were moving fast for jobs that require vocational training.

"While hourly wages in the broad category of maintenance and repair workers rose 6.4 percent from 2007 to 2010, increases were 10 percent in the subcategory of heavy-vehicle mechanics and 15 percent for specialists in electrical repairs on commercial and industrial equipment. The implication is that employers were competing for a limited pool of qualified workers."[17]

In late 2012, the Boston Consulting Group studied wage pressure and vacancy rates in the manufacturing sector, an area reportedly hit hard by current skill shortages. Countering a report suggesting the manufacturing skills gap in the U.S. amounted to a shortage of 600,000 workers, BCG found that the gap was far less pervasive, estimating a nationwide shortage of 80,000 to 100,000 workers.[18] "The problem is very localized," said Harold Sirkin, the coauthor of the research. "It's much less of an issue in larger communities, where supply and demand evens out more efficiently thanks to the bigger pool of workers." However, BCG notes that because of additional growth and the fact that the average skilled manufacturing worker is 57 years old, the manufacturing skills gap could balloon to nearly a million in the next decade.[19]

Companies that fail to offer competitive wages, however, are likely to exacerbate their talent shortages. We're seeing wages go up in certain niche sectors. But for most Americans, wages are fairly flat. If it's truly a necessary position, a company should pay the necessary price.

NAVIGATING AND CLOSING THE SKILLS GAP

We mentioned earlier that nearly eight in ten businesses are concerned at some level by an emerging skills gap. What's interesting, however, is that only four in ten employers say their company is currently doing something to alleviate it. This is as surprising as it is significant. In many cases, HR departments simply don't have the resources they need to enact recruiting strategies or implement training programs that they know will help their cause. An unfortunate irony of the recession is that it simultaneously produced a need for high-skill workers while forcing many companies to cut back on the very people responsible for recruiting those workers. We hope to start a conversation that encourages companies to put human capital development first. The future implications of a growing skills mismatch are severe enough to warrant this shift in thinking.

To close the skills gap, it makes sense to start with an understanding of what employers think is causing it. We asked this question of hiring managers who expressed they were at least somewhat concerned about the gap, and the results, shown in the graph in Figure 1.3, reveal commonplace culprits: lack of science and math degrees, technological change, gaps in on-the-job training, and job requirements that are too specific.

Many of the perceived causes of the skills gap, such as education shortfalls or technological change outpacing skills acquisition, are

FIGURE 1.3 | CAUSES OF SKILLS GAP

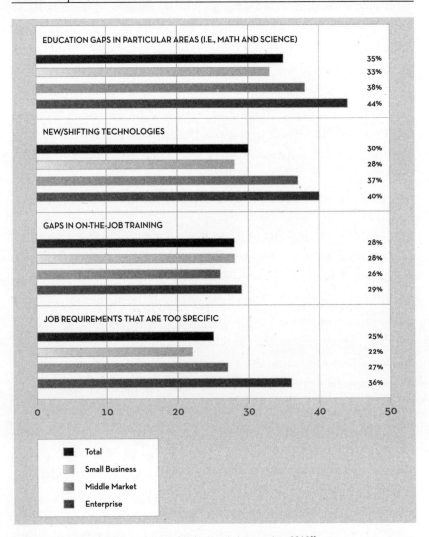

EDUCATION GAPS IN PARTICULAR AREAS (I.E., MATH AND SCIENCE)
- 35%
- 33%
- 38%
- 44%

NEW/SHIFTING TECHNOLOGIES
- 30%
- 28%
- 37%
- 40%

GAPS IN ON-THE-JOB TRAINING
- 28%
- 28%
- 26%
- 29%

JOB REQUIREMENTS THAT ARE TOO SPECIFIC
- 25%
- 22%
- 27%
- 36%

■ Total
☐ Small Business
■ Middle Market
■ Enterprise

Source: CareerBuilder Talent Crunch Study, Harris Interactive, 2012[20]

structural. In other words, their solutions require a broader discussion among companies, governments, and academia. When examining these issues more closely, it appears a large part of the skills gap is fueled by a lack of communication that can be addressed through a variety of solutions:

better vocational pathways for workers in skilled trades and manu-facturing; increased funding for research-backed workforce training; colleges and universities that better collaborate with employers about trending skills; and more employers willing to invest in training for elusive, niche skill sets. For instance, a community college in Indiana recently claimed that its manufacturing associate program was only 72 percent full despite a higher than average unemployment rate and local employers in need of more workers with these skills.[21]

Interestingly, employers do admit that some of the blame for the skills gap lays with them. Note that "job requirements that are too spe-cific or 'picky'" ranks higher than training gaps among managers at large companies. This should be an easy fix. If the recruiting and screening process is too idealistic in its expectations of the labor pool, the process can be retooled to give candidates who are mostly qualified a chance at employment. The problem is highlighted by a BLS study that found the average time to fill an open position increased from 15 days in mid-2009 to 23 days in early 2013.[22] The "pickiness" very likely represents broader economic uncertainty. Managers want the very best, and sometimes overlook candidates that would've been hired for the same jobs before the recession. We see this problem manifest itself in the common screening practice of only hiring people who have done the job previously. A 2013 CareerBuilder survey asked more than 2,700 HR and hiring managers if they primarily hired candidates who have previously held the same job title for which they are recruiting; 47 percent said yes. This makes it difficult for talented workers to make vertical career moves, and it also narrows the qualified-applicant pool considerably. As we'll see in Chapters 4 and 5, it's entirely feasible to screen out the perfect person for the job because of overly stringent qualifications.

So what happens when a hiring manager can't find the person with the right skills after months of collecting applications? The following are ques-tions we discuss with employers every day. The solutions are a roadmap to many of the issues discussed in later chapters, so we'll keep it brief here.

Do you have a continuous recruitment strategy? The easiest way to attack the skills gap is to tackle it before it affects you. Continuous recruitment means to collect a network of interested, qualified candidates even when you're not actively advertising open positions. Such a process allows recruiters to connect with skilled laborers who are already employed, but who may be open to making a career move down the line given the right opportunity. Inversely, building talent networks allows candidates currently in school or certification programs to connect with employers before entering the job market. But aren't costs a barrier? It would seem this would be the case for small or mid-market companies, but continuous recruitment is actually a cost-saving mechanism in the long run. We will discuss this process further in Chapter 6.

Is the skills mismatch for your vacant position a geographical problem? Employers must be familiar with the supply of skilled labor in their market. In many cases, skill shortages are hard to see when looking at national data—but zoom into the local level and talent shortages become much more apparent. For skilled positions, the employer's backyard is often the worst place to look. Recruiters with access to supply-and-demand data are better able to spend limited recruiting resources in markets that give them the best chance of finding the right candidate.

This is an area where big data can play a crucial role in averting the skills mismatch. In Chapter 6 we'll also look at workforce planning tools that allow recruiters to plug into regional supply-and-demand data. This empowers employers to be strategic about hiring decisions in ways they couldn't have just a few years ago. It can make the difference between months of fruitlessly waiting for the perfect candidate and relocating the perfect candidate immediately.

Are your wages and salaries competitive? The BCG manufacturing skills gap discussed earlier in this chapter found that when wages went up, companies had little trouble attracting skilled labor to fill vacancies. "Trying to hire high-skilled workers at rock-bottom rates is not a skills gap," the study concludes. Wharton professor Peter Cappelli likens this to car shopping. "The fact that I cannot find the car I want at the price I want to pay does not constitute a car shortage," he wrote in the *New York Times*. "Yet a large number of employers claiming they face a skills shortage admit that the problem is getting candidates to accept their wage rates."[23]

This has implications beyond the microeconomic level. If wages for highly skilled positions do not budge in the face of a talent shortage, it may deter workers or students from training in those areas. This is especially the case in manufacturing, where most skilled laborers are baby boomers who will soon retire. We must make sure skilled workers are rewarded.

Are you able to retrain workers for new skills? Ultimately, employers will have to determine whether the cost of vacancies outweighs the cost of training candidates themselves. The majority of job-seeking Americans are eager to learn new skills, but public funding of workforce training lags behind other industrialized countries and most employers are no longer dedicating resources to technical skills training. Clearly, many companies—especially small businesses—won't be able to institute technical skills training from a cost and capabilities perspective. But even if it takes government incentives, large businesses should begin to reinstitute apprenticeship-style training programs, where new hires work while learning new skills from their employers. CareerBuilder's tech headquarters, for example, hired 10 unemployed veterans and long-term unemployed job seekers with little technical background and taught them in-demand IT programming skills. Upon completion of the program, all but two were able to find full-time employment in the field.

DEPRESSING THE MULTIPLIER: THE IMMEDIATE IMPACT OF THE SKILLS GAP

A paper published by New York Federal Reserve economists [24] in August 2012 found that the skills mismatch accounted for up to a 1.5 percentage point contribution to the unemployment rate at the outset of the crisis. This may not sound significant when we're facing unemployment stuck between 7 and 8 percent, but keep in mind that the size of the U.S. workforce is about 155 million. Included in that number are the nearly twelve million currently unemployed. Even if the contribution of a talent mismatch fell to only one percentage point of unemployment, about one million more Americans would be working today. The spending power of that group would have a ripple effect significant enough to fuel demand for labor at all skill and education levels.

The ripple effect of job vacancies exists even on a microeconomic level. Hiring managers are voicing their concerns, in part, because the pressure is on them to fill high value positions first and foremost. A single unfilled job has a major effect on a company's ability to add headcount for lower-skilled support roles. Let's return to manufacturing as an example.

According to a 2012 CareerBuilder survey, one in three hiring managers in manufacturing say when they can't hire for a skilled position, it typically prevents them from opening up low-skill jobs or other support roles connected to that function.[25] Just how large of an effect could this have? There were 322,000 job openings in manufacturing in June 2012—up 50 percent from the prior year. As older workers in the industry begin to retire, this number could grow even further.[26] The potential losses in productivity due to skill shortages would mean fewer opportunities for workers in the back office and everyone up and down the supply chain. Overall, a dollar spent in manufacturing is directly responsible for an additional $1.35 in economic activity.[27]

In his influential 2012 book, *The New Geography of Jobs*, Berkeley economist Enrico Moretti describes how high-wage, export-serving industries like manufacturers or software developers benefit not only their own employees, but also employees in the resident-serving part of the economy—doctors, educators, small business owners, retailers, hospitality workers, etc. Hank Robison, senior economist at EMSI, told us that this idea runs counter to how we normally think about the divergence between high- and low-skill jobs. "It's becoming a familiar media story: while prospects appear increasingly bright for America's high-skilled, high-technology workers, competition from low-wage overseas labor is dooming America's lower-skilled workers to poverty wages and unemployment," he said. "But it's not that simple. The large multiplier effects associated with high-wage industries indicate benefits for lower-skilled workers, as well."

It's a virtuous cycle of growth: the better the export-serving industries perform, the more income its workers collect, which in turn creates a robust local economy. For instance, in his research, Moretti found that for every high-tech job created within a city, as many as five additional jobs outside the tech sector were created in both high- and low-skill occupations.[28] Similarly, data supplied to us by Robison and economists at EMSI shows that if 100 jobs were created in the Washington, D.C., biological product manufacturing sector, an additional 400 jobs were likely to be created through the supply chain or local service economy.

Robison told us that this is a clear signal. "Policymakers looking to vitalize their economies need to understand the implications of multiplier effects," he said. "In many cases, the best way to boost employment and wages for lower-skilled workers is to pursue industries otherwise known for higher-paying workers." This speaks to why talks of skill shortages or talent mismatches shouldn't be taken lightly. Even though the skills gap is by no means the top factor causing unemployment, it's a concern primarily for its ability to keep businesses from adding headcount for their most needed functions. The skills mismatch hinders productivity and innovation in a decade in which improving global competitiveness will be a top goal for U.S. companies. Companies must determine the source of their current mismatches, tailor recruiting strategies accordingly, and invest in workforce planning tools that can predict where mismatches could arise years down the line.

CHAPTER 2

An Absolute Good: Education's Value to Workers and Employers

There is no institution more important to the protection and development of a functioning democracy than education. This idea has been cherished for centuries and promoted by many of America's greatest figureheads. For instance, late in his life, in a letter to a prominent merchant and former U.S. ambassador, Thomas Jefferson touted education as a guardian of the Constitution:

> "I know no safe depository of the ultimate powers of the society, but the people themselves: and if we think them not enlightened enough to exercise their control with a wholesome discretion, the remedy is, not to take it from them, but to inform their discretion by education. This is the true corrective of abuses of constitutional power."[1]

Years later, in 1832, a young Abraham Lincoln promoted the expansion of education in his first public speech:[2]

> "Upon the subject of education, not presuming to dictate any plan or system respecting it, I can only say that I view it as the most important subject which we as a people can be engaged in ... For

my part, I desire to see the time when education—and by its means, morality, sobriety, enterprise, and industry—shall become much more general than at present ..."

And in 1938, on the eve of the world's most significant conflict, President Franklin Roosevelt spoke of the close link between education and free society. "Democracy cannot succeed unless those who express their choice are prepared to choose wisely," he said. "The real safeguard of democracy, therefore, is education."[3]

Decade after decade, expanding educational attainment has run in tandem with expanding freedoms. The public education system is the central piece of a self-correcting, constantly-improving democratic system, and has shaped not only the social landscape of the United States, but its economic landscape as well. The notion that education is an absolute good, we can conclude, is a self-evident truth.

However, in the wake of one of the worst global economic crises in history, doubt about the ability of the higher educational system to deliver progress—both for the individual and the economy—is creeping into public discourse. A growing chorus of commentators and consumers are questioning whether a college degree is worth attaining anymore. A 2011 Pew study found that a startlingly low 55 percent of those with undergraduate degrees felt college helped prepare them for a job.[4] Pessimism toward the institution that is supposed to be the primary gateway to gainful employment should give us pause. While many students believe you don't learn how to be "on the job" until you have one, we should still expect more satisfied customers when it comes to their career preparedness.

There's also the sense that the pursuit of the bachelor's degree is becoming a perfunctory, high-cost barrier to employment. As Caryn McTighe Musil of the American Association of Colleges and Universities told the *Christian Science Monitor*: "A bachelor's is what a high-school diploma used to be."[5] With more Americans gaining access to four-year educations, many people in this camp suggest that the once treasured bachelor's is increasingly irrelevant. Scholar and political scientist Charles Murray expressed in the *New York Times* that Congress should pass an amendment banning a bachelor's degree as a job requirement, calling it "educationally meaningless."[6]

We happen to know, however, that bachelor's degrees still have quite a bit of meaning. As we'll see in this chapter, the wage premium for college-educated workers, while tapering off, is still significantly higher than for workers without one. Better yet, recent research shows that cities with higher educational attainment rates tend to be more productive and have lower unemployment rates across classes of workers.

Some of the pessimism around the promise of higher education is likely derived from the poor labor market since 2007 and the challenge many qualified, experienced workers are having finding work. Students graduating during the recession did exactly what they were told—and many are graduating with impeccable academic records but are unable to land a job in their field. This is largely an indictment of the economy rather than of a failing higher education system, though. As the economy continues to heal, opportunities for young professionals will expand in kind.

The evidence in this chapter favors increasing access to postsecondary education, rather than uprooting the system. Along with that, however, comes the task of controlling ballooning costs for students, as well as designing curricula with the goal of improving employment outcomes. What businesses must understand, if they do not already, is that hiring more college workers is potentially worth increased compensation costs. In a study analyzing millions of career histories and thousands of companies, we show in this chapter that for certain job functions— management, sales, and customer service—increasing the number of bachelor's degree holders can boost a company's revenue potential by a significant margin.

However, there are obvious areas that could use reform. Graduating high-school students should more easily be able to choose shorter, skills-intensive degree programs or vocational apprenticeships for middle-skill jobs. The government must ensure a level playing field, so that students of all economic backgrounds have the opportunity to pursue the education and career path they deem best. Finally, employers need to collaborate more with colleges and universities to ensure curriculums are aligned with the current and projected demands of their workforce.

AT&T is one of many major companies sensing a disconnect between the workers they need and the workforce we may have 5 to 10 years down the line. Their Aspire initiative—a $350 million grant program designed to prevent high-school dropouts and boost the number of young students interested in STEM fields—is a welcome investment in school systems that are unable to make significant classroom upgrades and investments key to childhood development. We sat down with Jennifer Terry-Tharp, director of talent attraction and operations, and Julie Bugala, vice president of AT&T Global Staffing. Terry-Tharp and Bugala are on the frontlines of recruiting some of the nation's most in-demand positions.

"We are committed to education and dropout prevention, because we feel it's very important not only for our company and the future of filling our talent pipeline but also for our communities in our country," Bugala said, noting that more than one million students drop out of American high schools annually.

Considering one-quarter of AT&T's jobs require higher-level tech skills, it's clear they have a vested interest in not only increasing education attainment, but also sparking more kids' interest in the fields that will help their company grow years down the line. Terry-Tharp emphasized that while AT&T is committed to massive internal training efforts (more than $300 million annually for technical skills instruction), a lot of the individual workers' development will ideally be picked up through the education system.

"It's not about finding workers who know products. I can teach you about a product. It's about understanding technical architecture," she said of her need for employees with a hybrid skill set. "In order to understand the technology and communicate with increasingly savvy consumers, it's imperative even at the entry level—whether they're in customer service, a retail technician, or home installer—that they have a baseline level technical background."

That's what AT&T hopes to achieve through Aspire, which is the largest philanthropic investment in the company's history. Grants are awarded nationally to organizations that have evidence-based practices and data-proven strategies for improving graduation rates: school districts or individual schools and a multitude of nonprofits that share their same goals—like Teach for America, Boys and Girls Clubs of America, Girl Scouts, and Communities in Schools.

Education is, simply put, an absolute good. The university system remains one of the greatest U.S. exports and, provided looming challenges are dealt with, it will continue to offer pathways to higher wages and better opportunities for millions.

In this chapter, we'll look at education from two angles:

▸ First, we'll briefly discuss the economic benefits of a college education and the debate regarding the rising costs of obtaining a degree.

▸ Second, we'll explore the return on investment when a business increases the education levels of its workforce in specific occupations. In other words, we look at how book smarts affect a company's bottom line.

EDUCATION ATTAINMENT AND CAREER OPPORTUNITY

Despite persistent challenges in public education and rapid tuition inflation, the U.S. is still pretty good at granting more and more people access to higher education. In May 2013, the National Center for Education Statistics reported that the number of U.S. adults age 25 to 29 with a bachelor's degree or higher reached 33 percent in 2012, up from 23 percent in 1990. The number of 25-to-29-year-olds with a master's degree or higher rose three percentage points since 1995 to 7 percent. Better yet, increases in attainment are happening across racial boundaries: "From 1990 to 2012, the percentage of 25-to-29-year-olds who attained a bachelor's degree or higher increased from 26 to 40 percent for Whites, from 13 to 23 percent for Blacks, and from 8 to 15 percent for Hispanics." At every education level, female scholarly attainment is now greater than male attainment. More than a third of women (37 percent) in this age range have a bachelor's degree compared to 30 percent of men. [7]

All of this bodes well for the future of the U.S. economy. More college-educated women, diverse workers, and college-educated people overall are in the workforce now than ever before. However, if 36 percent of American jobs require a college education by the end of the decade, we still have work to do. But for someone weighing the decision to pursue a college education, a critical question remains: Do the potential economic returns outweigh the costs?

EMPLOYMENT AND COLLEGE EDUCATION

One of the clearest indicators of career opportunity is the stark contrast in unemployment rates of differently educated worker groups, as shown in Table 2.1.

At the surface level, there are a couple of things Table 2.1 tells us: 1) The recession appears to have affected each group significantly, and 2) you have a much better chance of being employed right now if you have a college degree or at least some postsecondary education.

Note that this chart doesn't show us what types of jobs people are in. A 25-year-old male with a bachelor's in management may be a barista— a job that traditionally does not require a college degree. It's likely that in

TABLE 2.1 | AVERAGE UNEMPLOYMENT RATES BY EDUCATION ATTAINMENT

Highest Level of Education Attained	Unemployment: 2007 (Workers 25 and Older)	Unemployment: 2012 (Workers 25 and Older)
Less than high school diploma	7.6	11.3
High school diploma or equivalent	4.5	8.7
Some college or associate degree	3.4	6.5
Bachelor's degree or higher	2.0	4.1

Source: BLS, Employment Situation Summary, Table A–4, Historical Household Data, 2007–2012

a low-demand economy, college-educated workers unable to find work in their preferred field beat out lower-educated candidates for even mid- and low-skill jobs. However, it's clear that one's likelihood of employment increases with education.

A 2012 study by the Brookings Metropolitan Policy Program illustrates why workers with little education are struggling in the labor market.[8] Of all online job listings in the top 100 metropolitan areas, 43 percent were available only to workers with a bachelor's degree or higher. (The caveat is that many lower-skilled jobs don't advertise online, so this isn't to say 43 percent of *all* jobs currently require a degree.) Less than one-quarter (24 percent) of all available jobs are open to workers with a high-school diploma or less—down from 27 percent in 2006.

This poses a simple mathematical problem: 40 percent of people ages 25 or older living in the largest metro areas have a high-school diploma or less. But the share of all existing and available jobs at this level was only 24 percent. Inversely, 32 percent of adults living in these areas have a bachelor's or higher, but 43 percent of job listings require at least a four-year degree. The final group, adults with some college education or an associate degree, faces a much smaller gap—making up 28 percent of the population and 32 percent of the job listings.

The gap between low educational attainment and quantity of job opportunities is wide and doesn't just hurt workers. Cities with high education attainment rates are faring much better than cities with low education rates. The Brookings report found a correlation between a city's education level and its ability to create new jobs. This calls to mind the multiplier effect discussed in Chapter 1. When a new position opens up for a highly educated worker, it typically leads to higher productivity, more entrepreneurial activity, and thus higher demand for lower-skilled workers. This explains why some major American cities thrive, while others fall further behind in growth and employment opportunities. The Brookings report found that "Unemployment rates are 2 percentage points higher in large metro areas with a shortage of educated workers relative to demand, and have been consistently higher than before the recession."

EARNINGS BY EDUCATION LEVEL

Earnings potential also increases with a college education. Those who obtain a degree, even in a blighted job market, will likely fare better than workers who do not. In pure investment terms, this is true, as well. Researchers at Brookings Institution's The Hamilton Project posed the following question: "If high school graduates had about $100,000 to spend (the average total cost of a four year college education), what would earn them more money over a lifetime: investing in the stock market or going to college?" They found that the rate of return for the average college graduate was 15.2 percent annually. Brookings scholars Michael Greenstone and Adam Looney broke down the comparison in a *Los Angeles Times* editorial:

"This is more than double the average rate of return in the stock market during the last sixty years (6.8 percent), and more than five times the return to investments in corporate bonds (2.9 percent), gold (2.3 percent), long-term government bonds (2.2 percent) or housing (0.4 percent)."[9]

On average, it appears a four-year college education pays off. This is distilled clearly when we look at a cross section of all college educated workers. Median weekly earnings of U.S. workers differ greatly based on the level of degree earned. The following BLS data includes earnings for all workers 25 or older in 2012:[10]

- Professional: $1,735

- Doctoral: $1,624

- Master's: $1,300

- Bachelor's: $1,066

- Associate: $785

- Some college, no degree: $727

- High school diploma: $652

- Less than high school diploma: $471

- Average for all workers: $815

The college wage premium is the difference in earnings between workers with a college education and workers with only a high school degree. According to research from the Federal Bank of Cleveland, the wage premium for full-time workers with a bachelor's degree or higher is about 1.8 times higher—up from about 1.4 in the early 1980s.[11] Although the premium has flattened over much of the last decade, it is clear that, on average, college provides the best path to higher economic returns.

EARNINGS BY MAJOR, OCCUPATION, AND DEGREE LEVEL

The field of study one chooses to pursue does make a difference—as does the occupation one enters after graduating. In 2012, the Census Bureau released new data showing what workers with various degrees can expect to earn over the course of a lifetime based on occupation.[12] While they are merely estimates and limited by a number of factors, the data show clear links between college programs and various career paths. Over a 40-year work career, the median earnings for a worker with only a bachelor's degree will be about $2.4 million. Workers who graduated with the following majors are estimated to make less than median:

▸ Education: $1.8 million

▸ Psychology: $2 million

▸ Liberal arts/literature: $2.1 million

▸ Biological sciences: $2.3 million

▸ Communications: $2.3 million

Workers who majored in these programs should earn more than $2.4 million over the course of their careers:

▸ Engineering: $3.5 million

▸ Computers and math: $3.1 million

▸ Business: $2.6 million

▸ Physical science: $2.6 million

▸ Social science: $2.5 million

However, observing median earnings by college major alone distorts the diverging career paths one may choose post-graduation. Occupation factors greatly into workers' estimated earnings. For instance, a business major who enters into an arts or media occupation is estimated to make $300,000 less than a business major who enters a sales-related occupation. Similarly, a psychology major who works in the health care space may make $600,000 more than a psychology major who goes into the education field.

Remember, the above Census Bureau study only accounts for workers with just a bachelor's degree. When we factor in the returns of advanced degrees, the wage premium only looks better. Presently, the median wages for those with a bachelor's plus a master's, doctorate, or professional degree are approximately 30 percent higher than workers with just a bachelor's.[13] Over the course of a lifetime, that adds up fast.

Like a bachelor's, not all graduate degrees yield the same returns. A study by the Georgetown Center on Education and the Workforce compared national median salaries of workers who went on to obtain a graduate degree versus those who stopped at a bachelor's.[14] For instance, business majors with an advanced degree earn $20,000 more annually. Social science majors and biology majors saw the greatest gains, at $35,000 and $30,000, respectively. The differences weren't as vast for journalism majors and arts majors, which were only $12,000 and $11,000, respectively.

ARE RISING COSTS A DEAL BREAKER?

Looking at earnings potential alone is only half the story. While the best economic data available suggest an investment in college is still a smart one, rising tuition costs are causing many families and young adults to reconsider. According to a report from Bloomberg, college tuition and fees have climbed 1,120 percent since 1978.[15] That's more than four times faster than the consumer price index. As a result, student loan debt is reaching unprecedented levels. Nationally, there are more than $1 trillion in outstanding student loans. The average borrower, as of 2011, owes $23,000. The recession added to these costs in two ways. First, states reduced spending on public colleges and universities, which prompted the schools to pass costs onto students in the form of higher tuition and fees. Second, students graduating during or in the immediate aftermath of the labor-market downturn often struggled to find jobs that allowed them to make any significant headway on their loan payments. As a result, the rate of borrowers who default on their loans within two years has doubled since 2005, according to the *New York Times*.[16] So even though college remains a smart bet for workers statistically speaking, it's clear to policymakers that costs may soon be reaching a tipping point.

Reducing the cost of college is one issue that has met a general level of bipartisan consensus. Everyone from conservatives like Rick Perry, the Republican governor of Texas, to liberals like Tom Harkin, the Democratic senator from Iowa, publicly rally against soaring tuition. Perry challenged state lawmakers to make certain bachelor's degrees available for a total cost of $10,000—an initiative 10 Texas colleges pledged to implement in 2013.[17] Harkin, meanwhile, stresses making costs as transparent as possible to students and families, which can include, as he wrote in a *Time* magazine op-ed, expanding "the number of those who are aware of the government's income-based repayment plan, which lets many students cap their monthly payments at 10 percent or 15 percent of their discretionary income," or directing financial aid to institutions with higher completion rates.[18]

The best strategies for bending the cost-curve will likely emerge on a state-by-state basis, and may involve a mass move toward web-based learning in some shape or form. For instance, MOOCs (massive open online courses) are free college courses with virtually infinite enrollment ceilings. Typically platforms for introductory-level, lecture-based courses, MOOCs allow thousands of students worldwide to interact and learn using crowd-sourcing technology, while instructors guide the course virtually through video and other technologies. The concept took off in 2011 after Stanford professor Sebastian Thrun taught an artificial intelligence course to 160,000 people worldwide. Universities are now lining up to offer courses through MOOC providers like edX or Coursera. As of early 2013, the future impact of this innovation is relatively unknown. But it could have the long-run potential to eliminate classroom-based, low-level courses if more universities begin accepting

MOOC certifications as credit. In March 2013, California lawmakers were already considering legislation that could force state universities unable to provide in-demand, low-level classes to accept credits earned in approved MOOCs. According to a Moody's investors report, the college business model could be upended if universities or providers are able to profit from courses through advertising or licensing fees, while keeping costs low for the enrollees.[19] This will never replace the need for in-class, physical campus learning. There are myriad academic and social benefits to the traditional university experience that won't be supplanted by online learning; however, when we're feasibly at a juncture when millions of students can simultaneously complete the same introductory statistics course through an accredited institution, MOOCs deserve to be at least a part of the cost control conversation.

WORKFORCE EDUCATION LEVELS AND MARKET PERFORMANCE

A 2012 CareerBuilder/Harris Interactive survey of more than 2,300 private sector HR managers and hiring managers asked which functional areas have the biggest impact on market performance. Predictably, the areas most closely tied to revenue generation topped the list, while other support areas that play a more indirect role with regard to market performance—legal, HR, finance—were reported as having less impact.

The following functional areas were reported to have the biggest impact on market performance.

- ▸ Sales: 33 percent
- ▸ Customer service: 31 percent
- ▸ Marketing: 21 percent
- ▸ IT: 20 percent
- ▸ Business development: 19 percent

The logic of the results is fairly straightforward. An underperforming sales force can be clearly tied to revenue performance. Likewise, an inefficient customer service system can be a leading source for drops in customer or client retention. Innovations in IT, new product offerings or acquisitions, and marketing campaigns can all be tracked and measured. These areas also command a large share of headcount within professional and business services companies.

The survey results vary along industry lines. IT companies, for instance, said that their tech employees had the largest impact (63 percent). The same is true for manufacturers, who tie market performance to their production workers (66 percent).

We asked this question in order to narrow in on a few important business functions, and subsequently figure out if overall educational attainment levels matter to a firm's performance. This isn't a consideration every company takes into account, because such data isn't easily obtained.

Generally, current or prospective employees obtain skills through either higher education outside of the workforce, or job experience. It's true, however, that different occupations have different ways in which skills are best acquired. In some cases, the skills must be built through experience; in others, skills are acquired through formal education. Oftentimes, it's possible to substitute on-the-job experience for education (or vice versa).

So let's get into the study by posing the key question of the chapter: For which job functions do education levels matter? The results hardly yield a simple explanation. To tackle this question, we tapped into CareerBuilder's extensive resume database and measured the career histories of more than 20 million professionals. To call this a deep data dive would be an understatement. But before we get into the results, it's necessary to discuss the methodology in brief, as well as why we think answering the question even matters.

A Note on the Methodology

Our analysis is based on two types of research. First, in a broad survey of HR managers, we directly asked what types of employees are important to retain, and how education requirements have evolved. (Note the survey question above, and the survey questions in the next section and Chapter 3.)

The survey results provided corroboration and motivation for a large-scale data analysis exercise where we examined how specific skills (measured by job tenure) and general skills (measured by education) individually or together affect company productivity in different occupations. We focused specifically on five occupational groups: IT, manufacturing, sales, customer service, and managerial workers. Our analysis relied on standard approaches for measuring firm productivity and sales value added, so the novelty of our data analysis is in developing detailed measures of the education, experience, and tenure profiles of workers at firms that participated in the survey.

Again, these measures were created by analyzing the career histories of more than 20 million workers and linking these workers to their employers through reported job histories. This is a highly robust sample, and to the best of our knowledge, is the only study that matches career histories with company market performance at this scale.

Note that it is difficult to tell from the correlations whether the acquisition and retention of more educated sales and customer service workers are causing changes in companies' market performance, or whether unusually high-performing firms are simply in a better position to attract and retain these types of workers. However, the broader evidence presented here and in Chapter 3 generally supports the survey-based evidence that talent acquisition can have a significant impact on performance outcomes. The regression-based estimates indicate that managerial perceptions are consistent with how firms' hiring and retention patterns are statistically associated with the firms' performance.

So even though we cannot assign a causal explanation to the results of the research, the consistency across the different sources of evidence reported here provides strong support for an economically significant and causal explanation.

We'll tackle the experience part of this issue in Chapter 3 on tenure.

SURVEY RESULTS: EMPLOYERS' VIEWS ON EDUCATION ATTAINMENT

In early 2013, we surveyed a nationwide, cross-industry sample of more than 2,700 hiring managers and HR managers about their views on education levels and hiring. While mixed, the results indicate significant preference for college-educated workers. First, we asked hiring managers about minimum education requirements for jobs they specifically hire.

- ▸ 18 percent of employers increased their educational requirements over the last five years.

- ▸ 44 percent require a four-year degree or higher and 54 percent require a two-year degree or higher.

- ▸ 17 percent have no educational requirements.

Note that the percentage of employers who require some college education is well above BLS educational requirement estimates. The shift toward a workforce more reliant on college-educated workers is supported by the finding that nearly one-third (32 percent) of employers are hiring educated workers for jobs traditionally filled by workers with high-school degrees. It's important to note, however, that part of this trend is a result of labor market conditions and college graduates' willingness to apply for jobs that don't utilize their new degree. Breaking this finding down by industry, we found that financial services and health care are particularly setting the bar higher by hiring more college-educated workers.

▶ Financial services: 53 percent

▶ Health care: 40 percent

▶ Manufacturing: 38 percent

▶ Sales: 37 percent

▶ IT: 33 percent

▶ Professional and business services: 31 percent

▶ Retail: 28 percent

▶ Leisure and hospitality: 20 percent

The key question here is whether employers are changing educational requirements just because they have larger applicant pools to choose from, or if they're seeing tangible benefits from being more selective. In other words, do employers see business value in this choice, or are higher education requirements just a convenient screening mechanism? Fortunately, most hiring managers and HR managers expressed the former position.

The survey asked: Has increasing the number of employees with a college degree made an impact on the following factors? The responses were as follows:

▶ Higher-quality work: 64 percent

▶ Productivity: 45 percent

▶ Revenue: 22 percent

▶ Customer loyalty: 18 percent

But remember, the majority of employers (68 percent) say they are not increasing education requirements for jobs traditionally held by high-school graduates. Nineteen percent of this group is not hiring more people with degrees because they can't afford salary demands, while half "don't believe it will have any impact on market performance."

With those trends and perspectives in mind, we can jump into the results of our resume analysis. Are there business functions that benefit from a higher-educated workforce?

SALES FORCE AND EDUCATION

Let's begin with the results for the professional area of sales. The key finding in our analysis suggests that education may be a substitute for experience. In other words, if you can't find a junior-level salesperson with experience, hire someone with a college degree. Intuitively, this should make sense to hiring managers for a number of reasons. Regardless of discipline or past work experience, we can assume most college graduates are proficient in a few intangible areas that translate well to a sales mindset—namely, the qualities of self-discipline and diligence, as well as the abilities to complete tasks in a timely fashion, socialize in professional settings, and work well with people of diverse backgrounds. High school certainly lays a solid foundation in these areas, but higher education theoretically prepares a greater percentage of its graduates for a business setting. In other words, a successful salesperson's skills may not be inherently related to 14 to 20 years of education, but it appears the additional time in the classroom helps. Companies that recruit a greater share of postsecondary degree holders tend to have better results, but to what extent?

Our analysis showed that a 10 percent increase in sales workers with college degrees is associated with about $31,000 higher value added per employee.[*]

This is a significant return on investment for a relatively minor increase. Sales jobs took a hit during the recession but have bounced

---

[*]Value added per employee is defined as (total sales − cost of materials) divided by number of employees. All data—sales, materials, employment, share price, and number of shares—produced by Compustat (division of S&P market services).

back in a big way post-recession. Many college graduates entering into the job market between 2008 and 2011 found that opportunities in their field were nonexistent or highly competitive. Some of this group took part-time work while searching for the ideal position. Others continued onto graduate school, while still others took a shot in an entry-level sales environment. Firms are eager to add headcount from a large supply of willing, highly educated workers. Whether or not the career paths offered in such sales roles are the best long-term fit for individual workers, an educated sales force is associated with a more effective sales force. While many junior or entry-level sales jobs are listed as requiring only a high-school diploma, our analysis suggests it may pay to target recruiting efforts to pools of new graduates eager to jump in to the labor force right out of college.

Looking at the growth trends of major sales occupations, we can pinpoint where college graduates will find more opportunities in sales. There are more than 23 million American workers in sales or related occupations, and just under half of them are on the retail side. Table 2.2 provides a look at part of the other half—those who fill the traditional business sales representative occupations. The data, compiled by EMSI, looks at expected growth in sales jobs on the services and wholesale side, which in total is expected to add about two million jobs by 2020.

While many businesses prefer a bachelor's degree, only securities, commodities, and financial services sales jobs typically require one.

Salaries for many of these jobs are well above the national median, meaning it's not improbable that hiring managers will find more and more college graduates interested in pursuing these expanding occupations. It is yet to be seen whether an influx of college-educated employees in areas previously reserved for lower-wage workers will also lead to increased wages for this group. If increased sales result, it should follow that labor captures a bigger share in terms of compensation.

TABLE 2.2 | GROWTH OF SALES OCCUPATIONS

Occupation	Jobs in 2012	Jobs in 2020	Change	Median Wage
Advertising Sales	224,910	241,127	+16,217	$21.37
Insurance Sales	1,013,006	1,159,300	+146,294	$22.00
Securities, Commodities, Financial Services	1,341,238	1,844,963	+503,725	$24.53
Sales Reps, Wholesale and Manufacturing (requiring no bachelor's)	1,688,396	1,850,820	+162,424	$24.85
Misc. Sales Reps	852,580	964,854	+112,274	$23.38
Models, Demonstrators, Product Promoters	175,103	182,573	+7,470	$13.00
Real Estate: Brokers and Sales Agents	4,299,554	5,181,330	+881,776	$15.25
Telemarketers	298,348	305,701	+7,353	$11.26
Door-to-Door/Street Sales	851,595	731,131	-120,464	$9.52
Other Sales Related Workers	402,741	455,248	+52,507	$17.52

Source: EMSI Occupational Data 2012

CUSTOMER SERVICE AND EDUCATION

Our study found similar results for customer service workers as those shown for sales positions. College-educated customer service workers appear to be associated with stronger market performance:

A 10 percent increase in the percentage of customer service workers with college degrees is associated with about $26,000 higher value added per employee.

But the findings may have different implications for the nature of customer service work.

Customer service jobs are one of the largest occupation groups in the U.S. In 2012, an estimated 2.2 million workers were customer service representatives. Over the next decade, these jobs are expected to grow by nearly 16 percent, to a total of 2.5 million in 2020, according to the BLS. We traditionally think of customer service jobs as being process and policy oriented—the fundamentals of frustrating customer service nightmares. In these encounters, which often take place after minutes waiting in a line or sitting on hold, customers understand they're talking to real people, presumably trying to help as best they can. However, customer service representatives often seem to lack the autonomy or flexibility to respond to customers' challenges in an empathetic manner. After a short on-the-job training period, customer service workers are tasked with responding to the inquiries and problems of their company's clientele according to neatly laid out guidelines. If they go off script, they risk losing their job. If they stay on script, they risk alienating the customer by not reaching a satisfactory resolution.

While this has been the historical approach, it is not the future of the occupation for U.S.-based customer service employees. Companies are finding wild success by running away from the traditional customer service model. Think about the online retailers Zappos and Amazon. Customer service isn't merely a department or function of their business—ostensibly, it is their core differentiator. In fact, CEO Tony Hsieh changed the entire Zappos inventory model in alignment with his values, as he explained to *Bloomberg Businessweek*, "We didn't want to sell just shoes. I wasn't even into shoes—I used to wear a pair with holes in them—but I was passionate about customer service. I wanted us to have a whole company built around it ..."[20]

If customers can't trust the product or service, why would they trust companies with their credit cards in the seemingly faceless online space? A rewarding customer service experience prompts consumers to shout their unexpected happiness on social media channels or write glowing reviews on consumer review sites. When customers are treated with respect or rewarded for their patronage, that's a place they'll go back to time and time again, often with friends and family in tow.

Because social media has become the world's largest forum for venting customer service horror stories, companies are investing in their own teams to monitor and track what people are saying about their brands to the world. Which is why, when someone Tweets about a defective product or writes a poor Yelp review, savvy customer service companies offer an olive branch to that customer within twenty four hours.

It is clear the evolution of customer service from a process-centered function to one that is more dynamic and involves critical thinking necessitates that businesses shift who they recruit to fill these roles. While further research that compares these new-wave customer service models with the traditional model is still needed, the results of our analysis may lend credence to this view.

MANAGEMENT AND EDUCATION

Hiring more educated workers for positions commonly filled by inexperienced workers seems to be a sound strategy for improving market performance, but does this line of thinking carry through to positions higher up the organizational chart? Unsurprisingly, the answer is yes when looking at management-level roles. Our analysis has shown that increasing the number of managers with bachelor's degrees is associated with major returns on sales revenue:

A 10 percent increase in management workers with college degrees is associated with an additional $63,000 value added per employee.

Management jobs typically require a broad mix of skills: deft interpersonal and organizational skills, a working knowledge of basic accounting, industry expertise, writing and presentation skills and, in most cases, proficiency or expertise in the skills the manager's employees are practicing in their roles. Recruiters hiring outside the company for management-level positions are most likely going to be checking for a degree regardless, but our study is further proof that there is a strong link between college completion and managerial success. Interestingly, the CareerBuilder survey of hiring managers and HR managers indicated that a significant percentage of employers prefer college-educated employees when making promotion decisions. Thirty-eight percent are unlikely to promote someone who doesn't have a college degree.

EDUCATION LEVELS OF MANUFACTURING AND IT WORKFORCES

So far, it seems that those suspicious of the value of a bachelor's degree aren't quite on the money, at least from the organizational perspective. Education levels of sales, customer service, and management workers are all closely tied to bottom-line performance, but is this the case for all functions?

Applying the same research methodology to manufacturing workers, we found a different story. Hiring more college-educated workers doesn't appear to differentiate companies. The correlation disappeared and our analysis showed no significant value-added effect for an increase in manufacturing workers with college degrees.

This probably isn't a surprise to many manufacturing industry experts. The current manufacturing workforce is much the same as in generations past. Production workers are experienced in their industry and know their trade. Many are highly skilled in their functions. But a bachelor's degree isn't going to affect the nature of the work. Manufacturing provides the classic middle-skill job, in which the expertise required is learned through training and experience rather than theoretical classwork. When workers want to move to the managerial level, the conversation changes, and college education is likely a major plus both for the organization and for the individual.

While education is not a good gauge of a manufacturing organizations' financial success at this point in time, that doesn't mean our research couldn't find completely different results 10 years from now. The manufacturing labor market is shifting heavily toward STEM workers, and newer, tech-focused manufacturing jobs are not just about learning a complex machine or process anymore. They often require hard skills traditionally taught in classrooms.

What may surprise people, however, is that the story is practically the same when looking at a company's IT workers. Once again, our correlation between increases in college-educated workers and the firm's market performance can't be found. There is no significant value-added effect for an increase in IT workers with college degrees.

On its face, this suggests that our push to encourage more students to enter tech and science fields is misguided, right? After all, if there's no apparent benefit to hiring more college-educated IT workers, where does that leave recruiters? As with most issues in high-value recruitment, there's no simple explanation. Our research is not saying IT education or computer science degrees are useless. It's safe to assume most workers in IT are college educated already, unlike those in manufacturing, customer service, and even sales, in some cases. For example, according to data supplied by EMSI, 75 percent of workers in computer-related occupations hold a bachelor's degree or higher, so a 10 percent increase in college-educated workers in this area at an individual company may not add noticeable value.

If anything, IT success is about continuing education. Skills change rapidly. Business tech needs are so radically different year-over-year that degrees aren't the best predictor of a tech workforce's effects on the bottom line. This is a major reason why salaries are increasing quickly for IT workers with in-demand skills such as mobile application development and the latest programming languages.

For this reason, hiring managers and recruiters should think twice before writing "bachelor's or higher required" in a job listing. Some of the top IT minds in Silicon Valley dropped out of college because lucrative entrepreneurial opportunities trumped the need to finish the degree. The major tech players in Silicon Valley send recruiters to campuses such as Harvard, MIT, and Stanford to offer jobs long before the best students don their graduation robes. In-demand computer skills are often self-taught, as well. This is one area where examples of work and evidence of proficiency should, without question, be on equal footing in the screening process for non-management IT jobs. If you've been waiting for the elusive programmer who knows Ruby on Rails, make sure the right person isn't being screened out of the process before a hiring manager can see what the person knows. Nevertheless, for all but the most adept IT minds, college still remains the best gateway to future employment, as well as the most efficient vehicle for acquiring other strategic and analytical skills useful to work in a dynamic business environment.

Also, boosting the number of IT degrees in your workforce is not the same as boosting the quantity of IT skills. Perhaps the best explanation for the lack of correlation between market performance and an increase of IT degrees has to do with the shelf life of tech skills. Prior work of ours (Tambe, Hitt, Brynjolfsson; Bresnahan, Brynjolfsson, and Hitt, 2003) found that firms that consistently invest in "IT-related intangible capital" (ITIC) such as new work practices and employee skills are more productive than firms that do not make such investments. The total size of these ITIC investments is large and growing. In 1995, ITIC was about 20 percent of firms' total assets. In 2006, that figure had risen to 40 percent. But companies have to be diligent on the upkeep of their workforce's skills mix. The research discovered that the mix of work practices and workforce skills depreciates at about the same rate as physical assets. Companies that fail to provide an organizational environment where their workers can learn and utilize new skills stand to lose their competitive advantage.[21]

To keep up with the high demand of difficult-to-fill positions, companies must be more agile. Employers can blame university computer science departments all they want, but expecting school curricula to keep pace in real-time with the constantly evolving demands of the IT business is not a game plan that will land them the mobile applications developer their company has needed for three months. Recruiters must keep a running list of their in-demand skills. What languages do your developers and engineers need to know? What emerging technologies might you adopt? Fortunately, the shortage of workers with these in-demand skills is causing many Silicon Valley firms to work more closely with university computer science programs, and leading to the creation of online computer coding schools that allow almost anyone to acquire new skills at a relatively low cost.

High schools and middle schools can also play a role in addressing this issue. The origin of Bill Gates' success is often said to be largely because he was one of the few primary school students in the country to have access to a computer lab.

More broadly, major employers need to do a better job working with schools and certification providers to identify the emerging skills that will define the IT labor market. Firms must measure the total cost of hiring a new IT worker and compare that to the cost of training an experienced tech-savvy person who's only a certification away from being the best fit for the organization.

Rising education attainment is, in most cases, beneficial to workers. Likewise, a more educated workforce is strongly associated with higher revenue when companies hire more sales, customer service, and management employees with bachelor's degrees. However, education is not the only way we measure how well a person can do a job. On-the-job experience, often acquired through a long tenure at a single organization, has long been seen as a natural way to improve a worker's performance. It is to this subject we turn in the next chapter.

CHAPTER 3

Tenure's Effect on Market Performance

The career path of Clayton Hollis, Jr., of Lakeland, Florida, is a quintessential outlier. In November 2012, he retired from Publix Super Markets Inc. after 40 years of working for the company. He had started at the age of 16, bagging groceries and eventually working his way up to store manager. After that he became director of public affairs, and that experience led to a promotion to vice president. Upon retirement, he told his local paper, *The Ledger*, "I feel I've had an unbelievable life at Publix—not a career, a life."[1]

His story evokes nostalgia for a time when going into the family trade was a real option for many young adults; Hollis's father and grandfather were both at one time leaders for the Florida-based chain. Loyalty to a company for a lifetime—or even the majority of one's career—seems hard to fathom for most private-sector workers. Even if we love working for an organization and wish to remain loyal to it, there are myriad life circumstances and career opportunities that cause us to change jobs.

What's harder to find is an entire organization full of people like Clayton Hollis. One such company may be the Illinois-based agricultural equipment manufacturer, John Deere, a company that is perennially a recipient of AARP's Best Employers for Workers Over 50. Not many major companies can boast tenure rates that make their employee rolls look like family trees, but John Deere is close. The average tenure of employees age fifty or older is 24.6 years—more than double the national tenure rate for workers at that age.[2] While the company is committed to recruiting and training a new generation of workers, it's clear that it considers retaining a strong and loyal workforce as equally important.

If such stories paint a picture of reciprocal loyalty between company and employee, you can bet that the picture is very different from the norm today. In this chapter we explore a simple question: Can you measure the strength of a company by the longevity of its employees' tenure?

The word tenure is derived from the Latin *tenere*, which means to "hold or keep." But its contemporary usage isn't associated with typical private-sector jobs. We most closely think of tenure in its academic or judicial context. Teachers, professors, and judges with tenure are guaranteed their office or position, provided they uphold their contract. By design, attempts to remove or fire tenured professionals are often costly and slow processes. The idea is that employment in certain professions should not be held to the whims of brash political decisions. For instance, teachers need a level of independence and don't think they should be fired when a parent disapproves of a book selection, or curriculum topic; likewise, judges need autonomy from special interests or partisan groups with political agendas. Running parallel to other labor movements of the time, teacher and professor tenure became a hot political issue in the early twentieth century and continues to be a controversial item in our national discourse today.[3]

Tenure for the rest of us simply means how long we hold a particular job—our length of service for a particular employer. Promotions and job changes within an organization do not reset the tenure clock. Typically, we hear tenure stories about individuals—the gold watch winners or the perennial job hoppers—and a discussion of whether that's a smart decision for the worker. We don't often talk about how tenure affects business. Sure, preventing voluntary turnover is a concern. Recruitment and training costs become a drag when churn is systemically high. We also frequently discuss retention strategies. But our goal is to explore whether or not an increase in average tenure can benefit a company. Put simply, long tenure matters more than you may think. Retaining teams for longer than five years is directly tied to market performance in some functional areas, but not for others.

So to fully understand related issues such as retention strategy, employee turnover, and career paths, we need to be grounded in an empirical analysis of workforce tenure.

- ▸ First, we'll examine employee tenure at the national level currently and historically.

- ▸ Second, we'll proceed to new research on tenure that could have significant implications for talent management. Long tenure is associated with higher value added for customer service and IT workers, but not necessarily for manufacturing, management, and sales workers.

LOYALTY TO COMPANY VERSUS LOYALTY TO CAREER: EMPLOYEE TENURE TRENDS

In late 2012, we asked a nationwide, representative sample of HR managers how much they knew about average employee tenure at their firms. We wanted to see how it stood up to government-collected numbers based on worker surveys. Here's what we found:

- ▸ 1–2 years: 5 percent

- ▸ 3–4 years: 16 percent

- ▸ 5 years: 21 percent

- ▸ 6–7 years: 13 percent

- ▸ 8–9 years: 8 percent

▶ 10 years: 9 percent

▶ 11–15 years: 11 percent

▶ 16–20 years: 7 percent

▶ 20+ years: 4 percent

▶ Not sure: 8 percent

While half of the surveyed HR managers stated tenure was between three and seven years, 39 percent believe their average is seven-plus years. This appears to be slightly inflated from government statistics. The most recent (2012) average tenure is, according to the BLS, 4.2 years for all private sector workers. Factoring in government employees, tenure is 4.6 years. On its face, this suggests that the average person will work for eight to ten different employers throughout his or her career.

The story of workplace tenure is changing for some segments and remaining very much the same in others. Figure 3.1 allows us to take a closer look at data from the past three decades.

FIGURE 3.1 | AVERAGE EMPLOYEE TENURE, 1983–2012

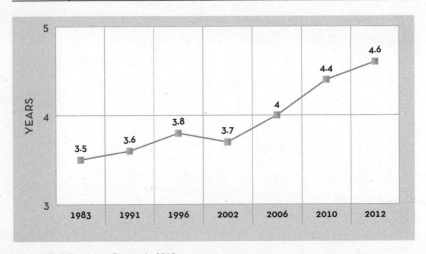

Source: BLS Employee Tenure in 2012

AVERAGE TENURE ON THE RISE

The BLS data indicates that tenure has lengthened by one year since 1983, mainly fueled by slow growth in the last decade. Figure 3.1 tracks tenure averages of all wage and salary earners. Until the 2001 recession, average tenure had remained fairly stable. Employees stayed at their firms for about 3.5 years or slightly longer before moving to a new job. For instance, tenure in 2002 was only two-tenths of a year longer than it was in 1983. But in the 10 years from 2002 to 2012, the national average rose by about one year. The climb continued through the 2007 recession. Average tenure was 4 years in 2004 and 2006. By 2010, it had jumped to 4.4, and by 2012 to 4.6.[4]

It's hard to definitively look at this data and point to a single cause for the increase. Part of it is simply demographic. The U.S. workforce is aging, which naturally pushes the average up. But the state of the economy plays a major role as well. In weak labor markets, voluntary turnover rates start to fall, meaning that workers' confidence about their employment prospects elsewhere shrink in the face of economic reality. We can call it the "greener pastures" test: If the landscape isn't promising, don't pack your desk. Even in the years before the 2008 crisis, when unemployment hovered around 5 percent, monthly job creation wasn't impressive by historical standards. The first decade of the millennium was wrought with political and economic uncertainty that may have contributed to rising tenures. Workers who had jobs, even if they wanted a better one, were reticent to quit before securing another opportunity. Once the country entered the 25-month period of job loss beginning in 2008, most employed Americans were hoping they weren't the next to lose their job; many hadn't even begun to think about what job they'd want to move to next. During the crisis, workers with less seniority were often the first to be laid off, driving tenure rates up. At the same time, many seniors delayed retirement, which also increased tenure. This was true for workers of all skill levels and education backgrounds.

FIGURE 3.2 | BLS DATA ON AVERAGE TENURE, SHOWING GENDER DIFFERENCES AND
AVERAGE LENGTH OF TENURE IN THE PUBLIC AND PRIVATE SECTORS

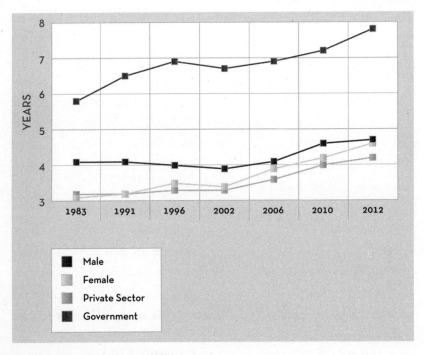

Source: BLS Employee Tenure in 2012

AVERAGE TENURE AND GENDER

According to data from BLS, the tenure gap between men and women closed in the last decade, as shown in Figure 3.2. In the early 1980s, women were continuing to enter the workforce in high numbers. The labor force participation rate of working-age women over the age of 20 increased from 51.3 percent in 1980 to 59.2 percent at the end of 2012. In real numbers, that means if the participation rate had stayed at the 1980s level, there would be about nine million fewer women working today. We're seeing the inverse trend with men, however: the participation rate in 1980 was about 80 percent for men over 20. Today it has fallen to roughly 73 percent. While there is still a greater share of men than women in the workforce relative to their populations, women are now working jobs just as long as men, indicating fewer women are leaving the workforce for marriage or children, and more and more are finding better career path opportunities within their companies. Considering the fact women are entering and completing college at higher rates, this shouldn't come as a surprise.

PRIVATE AND PUBLIC SECTOR TENURE

As can also be seen in Figure 3.2, the stark divide between private and public sector tenure continues. You probably noticed the line soaring over the other tenure measures in Figure 3.2. This is the tenure of government employees. It exceeds the tenure rate for the private sector by more than 3.5 years. This gap has always existed. While both tenure in the private and public sectors rose significantly over the past decade, the difference is mostly explainable by the nature of government work: A police officer, educator, or other city worker is much more likely to stay with the same employer than is a private sector professional. Unless they move cities, leave the labor force, or make a switch into the private sector, it makes sense that a government worker would have a longer term of service. And let's not forget, government jobs are one of the increasingly few places workers will find traditional pension programs, despite the fiscal turmoil felt in many states and localities. While this explains current tenure trends, it is all likely to change amid ongoing reform movements and pension crises in many states.

ARE YOUNGER WORKERS JOB HOPPERS?

It has become a popular myth that younger workers are becoming opportunistic job hoppers. There seems to be a sense that Millenials expect instant gratification when it comes to their careers; that they won't stay in a job too long without progression. Some believe they don't form enduring loyalties to employers—that they're willing to jump from company to company until they achieve a position they desire. Much of this sentiment *is* true. A September 2012 CareerBuilder study of generational differences in the workplace found that there is a significant philosophical difference on the topic of career progression.[5] The study showed that younger workers tend to view a career path with a "seize any opportunity" mindset, while older workers are more likely to place value in loyalty and putting in the years before advancement. When asked if they should stay in a job for at least three years, 53 percent of respondents aged 25 to 34 responded yes, while 62 percent of those over age 55 felt that this was important. A different question asked whether respondents believed that they should stay in a job until they learn enough to move ahead. In this case, 47 percent of the 25- to 34-year-old age group saw this in a positive light, while only 38 percent of the over-55 respondents indicated approval of this mindset. Similar contrasts were found when looking at promotions: 61 percent of the Millenials felt that they should be promoted every two to three years if they were doing a good job, while only 43 percent of those over 55 saw job progression in the same light.

What's interesting, and off-base, however, is the idea from some commentators that this behavior is new to the current generation of young professionals. Here's what an HR consultant recently told the tech website, IT Business Edge:[6]

"We used to tell people that they would likely go through seven or eight jobs during a thirty-year career. Well, that's now old news. In today's world of work—in the twenty-first century—people are likely to go through fifteen or twenty job changes during a fifty-year career. To put it another way, they are now likely to be changing jobs every three years or so."

Keep in mind, tenures are actually lengthening on average. But for the moment, let's only take a look at people relatively early into their careers. This can be graphically portrayed by the data shown in Figure 3.3, specifically the line for 25- to 34-year-old workers.

The truth is that younger professionals have always had short tenures. Tenure rates for 25- to 34-year-old workers have remained at

FIGURE 3.3 | AVERAGE TENURE AND THE AGE GAP

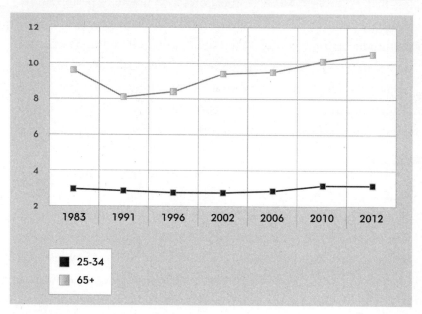

Source: BLS Tenure, 2012

around three years for the past three decades. Not shown here is the line for 20- to 24-year-olds, whose tenure has been consistently between 1 and 1.5 years over this period. In this case, short tenure can most easily be explained by young people taking on different jobs or professional internships during college. Moreover, very few workers post-college settle down at one organization until their thirties. So it's important to correct any literature heralding the emergence of a transient workforce of young professionals. This age group has been mobile for a while now, and that will likely remain the case in the foreseeable future. What might, in fact, be changing is the recruiting world's opinion of the job hopper.

The HR press and blog universe is home to a vibrant debate about the pros and cons of recruiting young professionals who don't seem to stay in a job for more than a year. Workforce intelligence company, Evolv, studied data of more than 20,000 hourly employees, finding that "evaluating applicants based on whether they had held multiple jobs for less than six months has no correlation to job tenure or performance."[7] Penelope Trunk of *CBS Moneywatch* contends that job hoppers are often motivated high performers: "You can't job hop if you don't add value each place you go. That's why job hoppers are usually overachievers on projects they are involved in; they want something good to put on their resume. So from employers' perspective, this is a good thing. Companies benefit more from having a strong performer for eighteen months than a mediocre employee for twenty years."[8]

But you can imagine hiring managers' anxiety if they had to fill seats every 18 months for key positions, which is why reservations still exist in many circles. Tech entrepreneur and influential blogger, Mark Suster, wrote a controversial post that was published on *Business Insider*, bluntly titled "Never hire job hoppers. Never. They make terrible employees." As a business owner with experience in startups, he plainly made the case for hiring people who value loyalty to the company in a volatile industry. Defending this sentiment from critics he said, "Quitting one to two jobs early when you're young is acceptable. I get that when people are young they're exploring life and work. But six times is a pattern."[9]

Staying with a job for three years is, in most cases, enough time for a young professional to decide whether to stay on an internal career path or upgrade their role and position externally. However, if it's clear a job isn't giving the individual the needed skills, constructively utilizing existing skills, or is actually an impediment to achieving career goals, that may be enough reason to look elsewhere in the first two years. Job hopping for highly skilled professionals is often a sound way to achieve higher salaries earlier into one's career. (Although, companies will do almost anything to keep these workers once they arrive.)

An important thing to understand about the low tenure rate for young professionals is that it may be pushed downward for economic reasons as well. Many college graduates seize on the first employment opportunity they get, regardless of whether it's in their chosen discipline. This is particularly the case in weak labor markets. It may take workers two or three jobs to find one that works for them.

However, the average worker probably won't reach 15 to 20 job changes, because careers gradually begin to take root and tenure begins to increase. By the time workers reach retirement, they've likely been at their current employer for more than 10 years, as you can see in Figure 3.3. And, according to a July 2012 press release:

> "The average person born in the latter years of the baby boom (1957–1964) held 11.3 jobs from age eighteen to age forty-six, according to the U.S. Bureau of Labor Statistics. Nearly half of these jobs were held from ages eighteen to twenty-four."[10]

Since 2006, median tenure has increased 1.5 years for workers 65 years and older. The financial crisis hit workers nearing retirement hard, causing many to defer retirement indefinitely.

TENURE'S EFFECT ON A COMPANY'S BOTTOM LINE

Now that we have an understanding of what the tenure picture looks like today, let's turn to how average length of service may affect your business. We poured through millions of job histories in CareerBuilder's resume database, connecting tenure averages with a company's market performance. The robustness of the data—which includes virtually countless positions for jobs in a multitude of occupations and geographic areas—allows us to make statistically valid associations between length of service and the value it does or does not bring to a company.

First, it's important to place our results in the context of how managers connect tenure with productivity and market performance.

Remember that our survey of HR managers found that half of American workers leave their job in seven years or less, on average. It's hard to say whether this is a good thing or not. Does it pay off when workers are more loyal? The answer to that question can significantly affect how companies approach retention and workforce management policies. We asked the same managers which workers tend to be the most productive, as measured by length of service.

Table 3.1 suggests companies are basically getting it right. More than half of hiring managers say the most productive workers are those who have been on the job between three and seven years. In other words, these employers are in good shape in terms of retaining workers they deem productive. The results are similar when we asked which workers have the greatest impact on market performance.

Again, as shown in Table 3.2, years three to seven seem to be the sweet spot for tenure, especially years three to five. The first two years are used to ramp up and assess an employee's potential. By the third year, managers see a spike in productivity and, in turn, tangible results.

TABLE 3.1 | TENURE AND WORKER PRODUCTIVITY

10%	24%	19%	12%	7%	11%	8%	4%	6%
1-2 yrs.	3-4 yrs.	5 yrs.	6-7 yrs.	8-9 yrs.	10 yrs.	11-15 yrs.	16-20 yrs.	20+ yrs.

Source: CareerBuilder/Harris Interactive Employer Survey 2012

TABLE 3.2 | WORKER TENURE AND MARKET PERFORMANCE

8%	19%	21%	13%	8%	12%	8%	5%	7%
1-2 yrs.	3-4 yrs.	5 yrs.	6-7 yrs.	8-9 yrs.	10 yrs.	11-15 yrs.	16-20 yrs.	20+ yrs.

Source: CareerBuilder/Harris Interactive Employer Survey 2012

But this data raises several important questions. We'll address each through the results and implication of our research.

▸ If managers sense employees with longer tenures aren't as productive or critical to market performance, do managers have the mechanisms in place to prevent any decline in performance?

▸ Are there certain functions in which it's ideal to have a greater percentage of your workforce with longer tenures?

▸ What are the potential consequences when an employee leaves in the three-to-five year time frame?

When a key employee leaves early in her tenure, it can lead to lost revenue, costly vacancies, and lower productivity. But we specifically wanted to know the areas where this was most felt. We asked hiring managers in which functions they saw the greatest negative impact on market performance if an employee leaves within five years. The responses were as follows:

▸ Customer service: 24 percent

▸ Sales: 20 percent

▸ IT: 14 percent

▸ Business development: 13 percent

▸ Manufacturing: 10 percent

▸ Marketing: 8 percent

▸ Human resources: 7 percent

▸ Admin/clerical: 7 percent

These results are very similar to the list of functions most integral to market performance discussed in Chapter 2. Employees in front-line, revenue-driving functions are essential to positive results.

The percentages change slightly depending on the industry. Naturally, not all firms rely heavily on production workers, but managers in manufacturing see their front-line laborers as the most important to retain for five years or longer. Overall, losing a customer service representative within their first five years has the greatest negative impact on market performance. The next function is sales, followed by IT and business development.

If hiring managers are correct, we should be able to find a connection between tenure and performance in the results of our study. As in Chapter 2, we looked at the most easily observable functions in our resume data: customer service, IT, sales, manufacturing, and management. While there does appear to be a strong connection between customer service success and length of service, that's not the case for some functions.

TENURE AND CUSTOMER SERVICE WORKERS

A 10 percent increase in the number of customer service workers who stay with the firm at least five years is associated with about an additional $16 million in value added.*

If you browse company website "About" sections, chances are you'll see a lot of bragging about extraordinary customer service solutions. Many tout the fact that their representatives have ample experience in the industry and, as a result, will be able to meet clients' unique needs efficiently. According to our study, such statements are not your run-of-the-mill marketing puffery. As stated, an increased share of customer service professionals with at least five years of tenure is connected to about $16 million in value added.

Whether consumer-facing or B2B, how a customer service representative responds to client issues is pivotal to winning repeat business. Experience is meaningful in the customer service space. Solving client needs

---

*Value added is defined as (total sales − cost of materials) divided by number of employees.

without being able to draw from a mental archive of similar issues and company best practices puts green customer service reps at a severe disadvantage. Consider a client who has used a particular vendor for decades. The client is a natural expert. When a product or service fails, the customer is accustomed to having it fixed quickly. An encounter with a customer service representative who doesn't know the product half as well as the client or doesn't understand the industry language will inevitably threaten the relationship. As we learned in Chapter 2, recruiting highly educated customer service reps is a great alternative, but overall performance very well may improve in conjunction with your team's experience.

The strong association between tenure and market performance is strengthened by our survey results. Remember, one-quarter of hiring and HR managers nationwide (the largest percentage in our survey) say losing customer service workers in the first five years has the largest negative impact. This is something that many in HR intuitively already know. Letting skilled customer service representatives leave or failing to reward high performance can potentially harm your firm's overall ability to address client challenges. But the added value experienced workers bring should convince more leaders to cultivate career paths for their best customer service representatives.

TENURE AND IT WORKERS

A 10 percent increase in the number of IT workers who stay with the firm at least five years is associated with about $11 million additional in value added.

Over the past 10 years, tenure has lengthened dramatically for in-demand, high-skill positions. BLS data shows that IT tenure is lengthening relative to other occupations. With increasing talent deficits, companies have been more eager to retain high performers. The two occupations with the highest growth in tenure from 2002 to 2012, according to the BLS, were computer/mathematical and architecture/engineering occupations. Tenure in jobs in these areas rose from 1.6 years and 1.8 years to a total of 4.8 and 7.0 years, respectively.

There's a scarcity of tech talent, and as a result, retention efforts have been redoubled in this area. Now we have data to back up what HR has long assumed to be true: losing IT workers early into their tenure can hurt the benefits in value added. If an IT employee can be retained for more than five years, recruitment costs can be reduced and organizations are able to maximize the creative contributions of tech talent. Hiring a highly skilled IT worker can cost a lot of money—and costs can reach an astronomical level in companies with high turnover rates. The cost of one extended vacancy can significantly downgrade an entire department's ability to function at its highest level. As a result, employers are extremely concerned their best workers will flee. A late 2012 Career-Builder survey found that 54 percent of IT firms are concerned top workers will leave as the economy improves. This percentage is 16 points above the average for all industries. The reason for the industry disparity is simple: Rapid developments in the tech world can set off bidding wars over talent. A skilled developer can either be with you or with the competitor nipping at your heels. It's no wonder achieving higher tenure rates is a valuable goal.

Interestingly, however, a past study of ours (Tambe and Hitt) found that job hopping in the IT world can have a positive impact on geographic markets as a whole.[11] Losing top IT talent within a few years can hurt industry leaders, but it is actually a boon to their competitors. This isn't as malicious as it sounds. Firms in the study were unable to simply get a free ride from the intellectual investments of leading firms. First, they had to build and invest in the necessary IT infrastructure to capture the spillover of talent from other firms. Technology laggards receive the greater gains because they receive all the benefits of "spill-ins," but face reduced consequences from "spill-outs" as their IT employees leave.

Let's think about why this might be so. If your organization needs to overhaul its strategy or innovate its way to market growth, what would the process look like? Knowledge acquisition can come in a number of forms. You might hire a consulting firm or you may choose to invest in networking and computer infrastructure to increase both capabilities and capacity. But in IT, a large share of an organization's capabilities comes from human capital. Infusing the organization with new talent can exponentially increase what the organization is capable of achieving.

We're essentially seeing an industry brain share, in which poaching the competitors' talent in effect raises the overall innovative capacity of the market. This is particularly the case within tech clusters in geographic areas like Silicon Valley, characterized by a high density of software, web, and computer companies. This explains why so many cities are attempting to lure tech startups by the droves. Pooling resources works to improve the labor market of an entire region and, in turn, its economy. As we learned in Chapter 1, successful tech ventures create high-paying jobs, which in turn create demand for other resident-serving service jobs.

For example, New York City mayor Michael Bloomberg launched a major initiative to showcase the region as a growing digital hub. His office, in partnership with a network of more than 500 startups and investors, created an interactive map (madeinny.com) pinpointing the locations of thousands of available tech jobs in Manhattan and the boroughs. In October 2012, Mayor Rahm Emanuel of Chicago announced ChicagoNEXT, a council of local business leaders whose goal is to attract new capital in the digital, clean technology, and life sciences sectors. Some companies are even working together to share tech recruitment costs. The Austin Technology Council launched a program in which eight companies paid contractors to scour universities nationwide for top tech prospects. The companies then shared the list and pursued the candidates on their own.

The point of it all: It pays to retain top tech employees, but competitors, or firms that employ similar skill sets can also be an important ally in finding, recruiting, and developing talent.

Tenure and Sales, Manufacturing, and Management Workers

Interestingly, our research found no additional positive correlations between longer tenure and increased value added in the sales, manufacturing, or management sectors. The clear associations ended with customer service and IT.

TENURE AND SALES WORKERS

There is no significant value-added effect for retaining sales workers for more than five years. This may seem counterintuitive. Wouldn't an average tenure of ten years for sales representatives be a sign that the company is probably doing pretty well? It may, but it likely does not, because the steady labor flow of sales workers to and from companies is a tried and true tactic of increasing market share. Having a core of experienced reps who know the industry, the products, and the needs of key clients is of course a good thing. No one doubts that. But if your company has no labor churn, you're potentially missing out on a lot of benefits. A new sales employee can bring leads, new clients, and fresh perspectives that can make antiquated tactics obsolete.

We have just discussed that longer tenures for IT workers increase value added even though firms frequently benefit from job hoppers coming from competing firms—so what's so different about sales? While nothing in our study can point to a conclusive reason, there is an important point of differentiation worth noting. Relatively speaking, the supply of needed IT professionals is much smaller than the sales workforce, both nationally and within firms. Sales is obviously invaluable to any company. Account managers and reps drive revenue through an intense passion for the business of helping clients meet their needs. Technology, however, is often the pillar of future growth—the organization's ability to create new products and services that adapt to market forces and consumers' growingly complex needs. The actual task of developing and building those services typically rests on fewer people's shoulders. Therefore, the challenge and cost of replacing a necessary tech worker may outweigh the costs of replacing a sales worker.

TENURE AND MANUFACTURING WORKERS

There is no significant value-added effect for retaining manufacturing workers for more than five years. This is of particular interest when compared with actual tenure rates for manufacturing workers. The tenure for this group is six years as of 2012, a full two years above the average for all private sector employees. A couple of factors offer us an explanation. First, as we noted earlier, the national manufacturing workforce is aging and we know older workers tend to have longer tenures. Second, within local economies, one manufacturer may be the backbone of employment for an entire community. If a welder leaves his employer in such a situation, there is often no other place nearby to go.

Even given these factors, we did not expect to find a correlation between tenure and productivity for manufacturing workers. If the person is trained well in most low- to mid-skill production jobs, they're likely going to do the job just as well in year three as they would in year ten. Because output and quality of work in manufacturing is more easily measured than in knowledge jobs like tech or marketing, it's easier for managers to measure performance. Length of service is not necessarily an indicator of quality. Our research isn't at all suggesting manufacturing workers plateau at five years or that it's best to achieve higher churn, but rather that excellent productivity can be achieved by shorter-tenured workers.

TENURE AND MANAGEMENT

There is no significant value-added effect for retaining management for more than five years. Management is yet another area in which longer tenures do not necessarily lead to stronger value added. Intuitively, you probably already know why this is true. The pressures associated with leading a team can be ill-suited for risk-averse managers. For some veteran managers, it becomes easier to choose the status quo over change. It's easy to fall victim to routine. It's easy to hire the same type of employees for predictability's sake. It's easy to keep the ship on course, but difficult to chart new territory. It's easy to constrict employees, but difficult to empower them. We've all probably had a boss at some point who comes to mind as this type of leader. Odds are they became rooted in such behavior as a result of a past strategy that worked. But without evolution and constant evaluation—resulting in an inclination to throw out the book and start all over—there's little hope high productivity will be maintained.

Successful managers learn from employees at all experience levels. They should promote autonomy, as well as exhibit it by changing course when necessary. Our study suggests not all companies are good at creating such an attitude of constant progression. This idea speaks to an important theme of any tenure discussion: Don't confuse longer tenure with better performance.

PERFORMANCE VS. TENURE

The implications of tenure data aren't as clear as the data on education. When recruiting higher-educated workers benefits your market value and sales growth, it follows that the degree is worth the price tag. Tenure is a bit trickier. When we talk about tenure, a discussion of retention strategy typically follows. Retention is part of the tenure discussion—and an important one. We'll cover retention in more detail in Chapter 7, but our data plainly shows there may not be a benefit to retaining workers merely for the sake of boosting tenure rates.

As we've discussed, out of the five measured functional areas, longer tenure is associated with higher value added for only two of them: customer service and IT. The first takeaway from this study is that it may pay to attract high-quality recruits for these areas and cultivate them. If longer tech and customer service tenure creates higher returns, rewarding these employees' loyalty is an advisable strategy.

In the vast majority of cases, rewarding long-tenured workers just because they've worked for a longer period of time is not a wise use of resources. Anecdotally, we can all probably name colleagues whose length of service clouded an ability to operate outside their comfort zone. At the same time, we all can also likely name colleagues whose long service with a company is inspiring, informative, and a true asset to employees of all stripes. The latter's length of service and passion for their role likely inspired continued growth; the former's length of service and loss of passion likely got in the way of it.

Of course there are many reasons to keep people besides stable return on investment: Rewarding loyalty with loyalty is a noble gesture; it's often easier to work with people who know the business; and it's reinforcement to the employment brand that you are an organization with which people want to stay. But also remember that longer tenure is not correlated with success in management, sales, or production roles. If a worker isn't adding value year-after-year, HR needs to be adamant in asking why he's still there. And if it's apparent an employee's tenure has reached diminishing returns, her role, goals, and responsibilities must be restructured.

Finding a balance between rewarding tenure and performance can be helped by asking a simple question: What is the career path for each employee at my organization? In an ideal world, every employee should know where they stand. Obviously, there can't be a clear and objective path of progression for every worker. Not every associate can be promised a corner office if they do X, Y, and Z in a set number of years—business is more variable and dynamic than that. A career path is a tangible outline of possibilities.

We don't suspect this line of thought is too radical or different from anything most HR leadership already knows. The system falls apart, though, without candor. In other words, a smart career path strategy isn't about keeping secrets from the employee. If a high performing marketing associate wants to move into senior ranks, she should know the odds of her finding the ideal position with her current employer. The last thing a worker with potential wants is work without a sense of progress. Inversely, her manager should know what the employee expects and wants out of her current role. Leadership should communicate where their employees stand, which options and opportunities are available, and how the employee can contribute meaningfully year after year. Annual reviews should be guideposts signaling an employee's progression, and perhaps every quarter, the manager should be considering these questions:

▸ Is the experience aligned with her career needs?

▸ Are her goals challenging enough?

▸ When will she reach the plateau point (the moment when her desire to take on more challenges trumps her desire to consistently produce in the current role)?

▸ How many years can we expect her to stay in the role before offering a promotion?

▸ If her desired position is not at our organization, is our relationship conducive to a candid conversation about her future?

No manager enjoys seeing a valued member of the team depart. But wringing out every last drop of productivity and creativity can result in negative consequences for both parties: It can leave a manager with an unexpected vacancy without a talent pipeline or adequate succession plan in the interim, and may stall the career momentum of a worker who has false expectations of promotion opportunities. If there's nothing else the employer can offer, there's no sense in maintaining a partnership in decline.

This is pretty basic stuff, but the point is that these conversations can't happen if there is not a career path program in place. It benefits managers to know the reason an employee stays in his job—not so they can force the person out, but so that they can help the employee through a restructuring of his assignments or help him take a new career step, either internally or externally.

So what does a successful workforce career path strategy look like? According to the popular metaphor first introduced by consulting giant Deloitte, a career path should function more like a lattice than a ladder. The problem with the traditional career path metaphor, the "corporate ladder," is that not everyone wants to or is equipped to climb it. A ladder's sole function is to help people ascend, but that's not a functional system for most workers. It's rigid. It doesn't accommodate workers who are happy to stay in their roles, but who may be able to assist the company in ways that stray from larger responsibilities and management. A career path that looks like a lattice, however, can be a chain of lateral, vertical, or diagonal moves through a company that makes career options more flexible. Even a move that is technically a step down in some firms is acceptable if the employee and leadership believe it's the best move. This approach allows firms to retain valued employees that might otherwise flee. It rejuvenates effective workers who enjoy the mission of a business but are burned out in their current role. Lateral moves are often the best option for a worker seeking a career kick-start, and they are often a necessary step before a worker can begin moving up.

*   *   *

At this point in the book, we've used data to look at human capital in ways not often discussed in recruitment strategies:

▶   The use of labor supply data in navigating potential and future talent mismatches

▶   The effects of boosting education levels on market performance

▶   The value added (or lack thereof) of long-tenured employees

These are large-scale exercises with broad implications, but we hope they encourage more HR and company leadership to measure and analyze such metrics at a scale appropriate for their firm. Finding, recruiting, retaining, and developing the right people with the right skills can be made easier with better data, and much of it lives somewhere in your server room, waiting to be mined and analyzed.

In the remaining chapters, we'll focus on more specific issues affecting recruitment and talent management that will be key to building a sustainable, competitive workforce in the coming years:

▶ Training and reskilling

▶ Continuous recruitment and pipelining strategies

▶ Candidate experience

▶ Emerging trends in retention strategy

In each chapter we talk to leaders at some of the world's leading companies. Everyone we interviewed for this portion of the book seemed to share one common theme: technology and data analysis are exponentially changing the way they find, hire, and develop their workforce.

CHAPTER 4

Empowering Employment: Training, Reskilling, and Hiring for Potential

In December of 2012, during the fifth holiday season of the Great Recession era, 12.2 million Americans were unemployed, nearly double the number looking for work six years prior. Undoubtedly, almost everyone in that group had a story of hardship, and a fervent desire to reboot their careers. However, there were 226,000 men and women included in that number that *no one* thought should be wondering when their next paycheck would arrive: the veterans of America's post-9/11 wars.

The unemployment rate for this group was 10.8 percent at the time—a full three points above the national rate and nearly four points above the rate for all veterans. There's hardly a soul in this country who does not support the troops, which is why it's disheartening to see so many brave men and women struggling to find job security having just returned from risking life and limb for national security.

In 2011, as this problem gained more and more publicity, politicians and business leaders began taking action. The unemployment rate of post-9/11 veterans was more than 13 percent that summer. Among the youngest group, those ages 18 to 24, the unemployment rate had reached 30 percent that October. President Obama joined executives from several large employers at a meeting at the Washington Navy Yard to announce direct action. The message: We can't let the economy be an excuse for letting our veterans down. Included in the initiative were tax credits for employers who hired vets ($2,400 for each short-term unemployed vet hired and $4,800 for each long-term unemployed vet hired.) The incentives were passed by Congress later that fall.

The president also challenged the private sector to hire 100,000 unemployed veterans or their spouses by the end of 2013. "If you can save a life in Afghanistan, you can save a life in an ambulance in Wyoming," he said. "If you can oversee millions of dollars in assets in Iraq, you can help a business balance its books here at home." Joining the President was Mike McCallister, chairman and CEO of health care company Humana. This major insurer and service provider, based in Louisville, Kentucky, has a rich history of hiring and working with veterans and their families. McCallister pledged to hire 1,000 veterans by 2014 on top of a $1 million donation to the Entrepreneurship Bootcamp for Veterans with Disabilities, a national program that provides training in entrepreneurship and small-business management at no cost to post-9/11 veterans.

We sat down with Carleen Haas and Kevin Stakelum, Humana's chief talent officer and talent acquisition director, respectively. Together with their team, they've been responsible for administering the veterans hiring initiative at Humana. At the time of our interview, the company had already hired more than 800 previously unemployed veterans or their spouses. At the time this book went to print, they had exceeded their goal of hiring 1,000, and, under the directive of incoming CEO, Bruce Broussard, are committed to hiring another 1,000 by the end of 2016. Stakelum, a veteran himself, was tired of seeing family members who had also served struggle to find employment after leaving the military. Now, glad to be a part of eliminating that frustration at Humana, he's impressed with the results. "I always thought that they were going to be great people, but when you see the impact that some of them are having when they come in—the new ideas, the new energy—you realize that they're not new hires, they're not juniors in capability," he said. "Their experience looks a little different on paper, but they're not people you need to teach how to survive in the workplace."

*   *   *

The nationwide effort to reduce veteran unemployment is a learning moment. If we can measure the potential of veterans and reward them with job and training opportunities, why can't we do this for all segments of the population ready to learn and be given a similar chance? This question has more than a noble premise. It's about securing an economic future that includes all Americans who seek to contribute. The long-term unemployed, be they veterans or mature workers, are at risk of being permanently left out of the workforce should their skills atrophy and their connections to the job market deteriorate. Without a concerted effort to reskill or simply give them a chance, the natural rate of unemployment could rise significantly, and a large segment of our potential workforce could go to waste.

What role should business play in getting the long-term unemployed back to work? How can the private sector empower employment by bringing more job seekers into the fold?

Many companies rightly believe that general-skills training is a risk. The apprehension seems to be summed up with the question: Why give a new worker a skill they can take to a competitor? This is a valid concern, and the truth is, some workers who are trained by an employer will inevitably leave. A company unable to retain workers for a significant period of time after training may not see a net positive gain. Therefore, training cannot be implemented in isolation. Clear strategies for development, career-pathing, and retention must coincide with training to ensure the candidates have incentives to stay. Fortunately, as we'll see, survey data suggests that offering training opportunities may actually be a viable retention tactic in and of itself. The modern labor market increasingly favors niche skill sets, so more companies should at least consider themselves as a potential outlet for facilitating training. If every employer capable of training for general skills decides it's not their responsibility, the very skills shortages hiring managers cite as a perennial concern will only be exacerbated.

Generally speaking, this chapter steps away from workforce analytics, supply and demand metrics, and job search and compensation data to look at the human element of America's unemployment challenge. There are so many talented, ambitious professionals who just need an opportunity to thrive—workers who've previously sacrificed time and resources to obtain an education but lack a missing piece on their resume; workers who've shown up to their jobs year after year, decade after decade, providing for themselves and their families as part of America's long-held, unwritten contract that if you work hard and want to succeed, you can. And yet, through no fault of their own, millions of workers lost their jobs and their economic security as a result of the largest financial crisis in 60 years. Many entered a job market that no longer needed their skill set, forcing them to start over in a climate that favored candidates who already possessed in-demand skills.

This chapter is about starting an organized, deliberate effort to reskill and train where possible. We'll explore the current state of employer-backed training, and share stories of how some organizations are developing their own efforts to empower employment:

- ▶ First, we explore Humana's continuing effort to hire more veterans and investigate how the efforts to reskill and empower this segment of the unemployed population can be expanded to include all people who've been out of work for longer than seven months.

- ▶ Second, we look at how American employers are (or aren't) training their own workforce and show how a reticence to train coincides with a reduction in government-backed workforce training.

▶ Third, we share the results of an experiment to hire and reskill long-term unemployed job seekers and discuss how some organizations are positively contributing to retraining and reskilling efforts.

THE VETERANS HIRING INITIATIVE

In order to figure out how to lower veteran unemployment, we need to understand why it's so high in the first place. Why are so many young veterans struggling to make the transition to civilian life?

An official White House brief gave context to the challenge:

"These veterans tend to be young and many worked in sectors that were among the hardest hit by the recession. Post-9/11 veterans were more likely to be employed in mining, construction, manufacturing, transportation and utilities—all industries that experienced significant drops in employment during 2008–2009."[1]

At the end of the first decade of the millennium, young men and women often returned home to see their local economies and personal employment prospects devastated. Adjusting to domestic life and maintaining mental and physical health can be hard enough for returning veterans; when they see that their mine or plant was shut down on top of that, picking up and moving on can be a very challenging task. Because hiring in blue-collar sectors has been slower than sectors that require college-educated workers, this leaves some veterans without many options. While many do go on to college, others seek immediate entry into the job market for personal reasons or to support their families.

Fortunately, those on Capitol Hill, working in conjunction with business leaders, decided that the extremely high unemployment rate among returning veterans was untenable. The efforts of Humana and other private sector leaders went a long way toward increasing awareness around the issue. Even when companies want to hire veterans or their spouses, it can be difficult to do so. According to CareerBuilder's 2011 Veterans Day survey, the biggest challenge when recruiting veterans, outside of assessing how their skills translate, is the fact that many veterans don't self-identify when applying for jobs.

This is something the Humana team recognized during the early stages of their initiative for hiring veterans. To help address this issue, the team set up a dedicated talent pipeline to encourage veterans to learn more about career opportunities at Humana without having to go through a full application process. During our interview, Stakelum explained that Humana had already hired a recruiter specifically targeting veterans. They eventually hired another. Both recruiters were veterans themselves. These steps were critical to the program's ultimate success, but they first had to convince veterans to be less reluctant to self-identify.

"Our approach is to be as upfront as possible as to why we are asking them [about veteran status]," said Stakelum. "Our message, even for their spouses, wasn't very clear. But once we were more direct in our goal, more came forward."

The second challenge for businesses is recognizing the value of veterans' service. More specifically, employers need to pay closer attention to the skills and experience listed on applications or within resumes. In other words, get past the headline.

"Most businesses recruit based on past [job] titles," explained Stakelum. "If you want a project manager, you look at someone who's been a project manager. If you want a consultant, you look for someone who was a consultant. But this isn't 100 percent effective. When you see a service member who is a tank commander or logistics officer, it's really difficult for the employer to draw that connection."

When encountering veterans who do self-identify, or any job seeker for that matter, hiring managers and talent acquisition professionals should take a moment before dismissing resumes that don't meet strict standards regarding past experience. In general, there are certain advantages for screening based on past or similar job titles, but you inevitably disqualify unique experiences and skill sets that translate well to the job description. "Past job titles are not always a good proxy for what it is that makes a person successful in a role," said Haas. "Leadership qualities, cultural fit and a can do attitude are often the best predictor of success along with the ability to learn."

In the case of veterans, companies are potentially missing perfect cultural fits for their organizations—motivated, quick-thinking men and women who have ample experience working in teams and achieving tangible objectives.

Stakelum says the hiring process is easier when veterans are able to draw connections between their skills and the tasks required by the job. "A lot of times the soldier or service member doesn't know what kind of things to put in their resume such as 'I led a team of ten, here are the accountabilities I held, here's the way I communicated, motivated and organized, and so on," said Stakelum. "Veterans don't always know best practices, but once they get to that level of detail [on their resume] successfully, it's not really much of a challenge for the hiring manager."

The 2012 CareerBuilder Veterans Day survey asked hiring managers to identify what they value most in veterans and consequently want to see detailed on resumes or in cover letters:

- Disciplined approach to work: 66 percent

- Ability to work as a team: 65 percent

- Respect and integrity: 58 percent

- Leadership skills: 56 percent

- Problem-solving skills: 54 percent

- Ability to perform under pressure: 53 percent

- Communication skills: 45 percent

Employers know veterans possess these skills, but if candidates are able to give shape to them and describe how their skills translate to the civilian working world, it makes the candidate all the more likely to stand out.

In 2011, the Department of Defense and Department of Veteran Affairs overhauled its existing career-readiness program for all service members, and initiated a mandatory "reverse boot camp" that provides resume writing and finance courses, as well as planning for college-bound troops, entrepreneurs, and workers who'll need certifications or other technical training.[2]

Stakelum warned that there's a downside to hiring veterans just for the sake of it. It can't and never should be a publicity grab. "In some cases companies try to force the fit," he said. "If you force a fit your chances of failure are going to increase. We haven't tried to find actuaries or other niche job titles. Even though every once in a while we do find veterans that possess unique skills, we focused on areas that were a natural fit for their service experience."

Haas, Stakelum, and their team identified five target areas or departments within the organization that would provide the best fit for the majority of their veteran hires: service operations, sales, marketing, nursing, and Humana Government Business, a unit of Humana that includes the wholly owned subsidiaries Humana Military and Humana Veterans. Veterans in these businesses were hired for a range of positions.

Once veterans are recruited to Humana, the onboarding process works a bit differently than for other new hires. A.J. Hubbard, Humana's director of diversity, launched a veterans' network resource group that specializes in acclimating new hires to the organization and the business world. "It's one thing to hire them and fill positions, but the network resource group increases the chances of them being comfortable in their role and adjusting to a business environment," said Stakelum. The program is run by Humana associates who donate their time on top of their day-to-day responsibilities.

Several other businesses and organizations are joining Humana to meet the government's goal of employing 100,000 veterans or their spouses by the end of 2013. Microsoft offered up to 10,000 free technology training and certification packages to veterans, and the U.S. Chamber of Commerce created a council of 25 large American employers across industries to promote veteran hiring and enact reporting measures. AT&T launched two new resources: a custom military skills translator that connected service members' skills with jobs at the company, and a mentorship program pairing AT&T employees with new veteran hires. In early 2013, Walmart pledged to hire any veteran who had left the military during the prior year.

The rallying cry appears to be working, but we have a long way to go. The average unemployment for post-9/11 veterans was 12.1 percent in 2011, but that fell to an average of 9.9 percent in 2012, according to the BLS.[3] In the first month of 2013, though, the rate shot back up to 11.7 percent. Unemployment rates for this classification of veterans fluctuate wildly. With operations in Afghanistan and Iraq winding down, varying numbers of troops return home and leave the service on a month-to-month basis. To capture any improvements in the unemployment rate, you must look at the overall trend line, which has worked its way down from above 13 percent to below 9 percent in just two years' time. However, the volatility warns us that it is not a challenge that ends the moment a static unemployment figure is reached or a hiring quota is met. The government projects that more than one million service members will leave the military between 2011 and 2016 as the wars fully draw down.

The lesson here is that hiring for potential works with veterans. Thousands of employers have decided to say, "I know this person can do the job." They are willing to give veterans a chance or allow extra time while their new hires ramp up to full productivity. They are willing to ignore that few of the candidates' past job titles matched their open requisitions. In many cases, talent acquisition professionals are more willing to train veterans for skills they might be missing due to lack of prior experience.

When this attitude is applied more widely, employers will take a huge step toward developing the skilled workforce they need and play a positive role in thwarting current or future skill shortages.

EMPLOYERS AND NEW HIRE TRAINING

As stated earlier, reducing the cost of and increasing access to college education and other postsecondary training programs is one crucial long-term solution for skill shortages. This would make switching careers and obtaining new skills much easier for a dislocated worker, as well as reduce the burden on employers. Any progress in increasing educational attainment requires employers or professional associations to be more closely aligned with the schools and institutions responsible for delivering skills training.

But there's another lesson here as well: To fix skill shortages in the near and long term, employers may have to play a bigger part in the training process.

The reality, however, is that limited training budgets are taking a back seat to other challenges HR managers have to address. Career-Builder conducted a representative survey of HR professionals in 2013, asking them to identify their top staffing challenges. Their answers clearly show how training ranks among other concerns:

▸ Being able to retain top talent: 44 percent

▸ Being able to provide competitive compensation: 37 percent

▸ Can't find enough high skilled applicants: 33 percent

▸ Lifting employee morale: 31 percent

▸ Being able to provide upward mobility: 31 percent

▶ Maintaining productivity levels: 26 percent

▶ Being able to provide competitive benefits: 26 percent

▶ Preventing worker burnout: 22 percent

▶ **Being able to provide training: 17 percent**

▶ Don't have budget to recruit: 11 percent

▶ Strengthening employment brand: 8 percent

▶ Allocating adequate time to recruit: 5 percent

We don't want to diminish the severity of these challenges. In fact, many of them are directly or indirectly related to retention, which we'll discuss at length in Chapter 7. But by looking at the list, we're able to glean a sense of what the priorities are for the average HR professional. It's clear the skills gap is of major concern, but interestingly, far fewer believe a lack of training opportunities poses a threat. We can read this a couple of different ways: Either employers are already satisfied with the training opportunities, or many companies don't have training programs, and thus are unlikely to cite it as a challenge.

In fact, training programs for most employers are either a) nonexistent or have been downsized for cost saving purposes, or b) primarily used to train workers for basic on-the-job procedures or company procedures such as safety guidelines or employee policies. Many companies claim they have training programs, but that doesn't always mean "We hire people and teach them new skills."

Let's take a look at what we know:

▶ Forty-seven percent of U.S., nongovernment employers either have no training budgets at all or have training budgets under $25,000 annually, according to a 2012 CareerBuilder survey.

> ▸ Twenty-nine percent of large businesses (500 or more employees) have training budgets exceeding $500,000.

> ▸ Thirty-one percent of companies (mostly small businesses) have never trained a worker with little or no prior experience for new skills.

A 2011 worker survey conducted by Accenture found that only 21 percent of employees said they've acquired new skills through company-provided training over the previous five years.[4] Interestingly, the final bullet in the previous list suggests 69 percent of companies say they've hired individuals with no experience in that occupation or field and trained them. That's undoubtedly a good sign. But this is mostly happening for low-skill positions, jobs that have a shorter ramp-up time and are far less costly to the employer to train. Of employers who hire and train workers with no experience, 66 percent primarily do so for low-skill jobs. Only one-third have trained new hires for jobs that require technical skills.

However, this attitude toward training seems to have begun changing in the post-recession, tepid-growth climate. Thirty-nine percent of U.S., nongovernment employers plans to train workers who don't have experience in the industry or occupation and hire them within their organization in 2013. Looking at large companies only, that percentage grows to 48 percent, according to CareerBuilder data. Research from Bersin & Associates found that corporate training spending grew by 12 percent in 2012.[5] On the other hand, small businesses, the engine of job growth in the U.S. economy, simply do not have the means to train all the workers they need. Moreover, they're not able to risk hiring personnel lacking key technical skills, regardless of their potential.

For the most part, companies believe the burden of acquiring skills is on the job seeker. This effectively places us in what Wharton professor Peter Cappelli calls a macro-labor stalemate, a situation in which "there is no training anymore ... businesses just hope to hire it in."[6] In early 2013, we asked nearly 3,000 hiring managers and HR professionals across industries and company sizes to state how strongly they feel about the following statement:

It is the primary responsibility of the job seeker to acquire in-demand skills through education, certification programs, or on-the-job experience.

▶ Strongly agree: 22 percent

▶ Somewhat agree: 44 percent

▶ Neutral: 25 percent

▶ Somewhat disagree: 7 percent

▶ Strongly disagree: 3 percent

While very few disagree with the statement, only one in five strongly feels skills training is mostly up to the worker. This leaves more of a gray area than we might expect, considering how many employers cite concern over the skills gap and how few lament lack of training opportunities. Generally speaking, however, a majority of employers think it's reasonable to ask job seekers to be the directors of their own careers. Even if it comes at a cost, avenues for skills acquisition exist.

We also know employers think schools aren't always delivering the quality of workers they need, which could be the primary reason employers may increasingly turn to internal training options. When presented with the following statement during the same survey, a majority of hiring managers and talent acquisition professionals agree they need to be doing more to increase their employees' skill sets:

Employers should do more to train workers for hard-to-find skills or offer continuing education opportunities that will contribute to a more highly skilled staff.

▶ Strongly agree: 24 percent

▶ Somewhat agree: 43 percent

▸ Neutral: 24 percent

▸ Somewhat disagree: 6 percent

▸ Strongly disagree: 4 percent

The fact is, if companies are not able to find the right people, it may be time to start grooming the right people on their own terms. But does training result in a positive return on investment for the employer? Measuring the effectiveness of training programs is very difficult, as the varying nature of worker training limits researchers' ability to observe and compare large samples. Moreover, certain benefits of formal training programs, such as employee satisfaction, are entirely intangible. Survey data suggests that despite its difficulty to measure, training is quite beneficial to the employer, specifically contradicting the most commonly cited fear of employers: trainee flight. No company wants to pay for continued learning or skills training only to see the recipient flee to a competitor. But training can in fact be a significant driver of retention and result in huge productivity gains. A 2013 CareerBuilder survey found skills training and learning opportunities to be a better retention tactic, according to full-time workers, than decreased workloads, academic reimbursement, and perks such as subsidized lunches, game rooms, or casual dress codes.

Bottom line benefits to training may exist as well. Researchers Mark Lowenstein and James Spletzer conclude that employers—even more than the workers—reap the rewards of training investments, finding that "the effect of an hour of training on productivity growth is about five times as large as the effect on wage growth."[7]

THE INSTITUTION OF WORKFORCE TRAINING

Gridlock over budget battles in Washington may very well shift the burden of training and development onto the employer or worker. In many cases it has already. In the spring of 2012, *The New York Times* reported on one of the more confounding skill shortages hitting several regions of the country: trucking companies can't find enough drivers. Atlas Van Lines, based in Louisville, Kentucky, sought to hire 100 seasonal drivers:

> "But a usually reliable source of workers, the local government-financed job center, could offer little help, because the federal money that local officials had designated to help train drivers was already exhausted. Without the government assistance, many of the people who would be interested in applying for the driving jobs could not afford the $4,000 classes to obtain commercial driver's licenses."[8]

Commercial truck driving typically pays a middle class wage. Even with the sacrifice of long hours and days away from family, it is a job in which we would expect to see long lines of applicants in a high unemployment environment. The upfront cost is actually a deal breaker for many job seekers though, forcing many trucking companies to operate under capacity or change the way they hire. *The New York Times* reports that Atlas lowered driving-hour requirements and offered a signing bonus. If that didn't work, they said they would consider covering training costs if drivers agreed to stay with the company for two years—an arrangement many companies make with employees when academic or training expenses are covered by the employer.

Employers who know about government workforce training incentives want to take advantage of them, but securing these funds can be difficult. The State of Ohio's Incumbent Workforce Training Voucher Program reimburses businesses or job seekers for certain training expenses. In 2013, $20 million was allocated to the program. Twenty-four hours after applications opened on January 8, the program received requests for $21.4 million.[9]

Federally funded workforce training programs have long been a resource for dislocated workers (those who lost a job because their employer moved, shut down, or reduced its workforce) and employers unable to find the workers they need. You might think that given the concerns around skill shortages and persistently high unemployment, there would be more funding for such programs. It's easy to point a finger at the recession and fiscal shortfalls as a reason for recent funding shortages. However, it's a trend long in the works, as shown in Table 4.1.

Workforce programs targeted to adults, dislocated workers, and youth declined by 55 percent in inflation-adjusted dollars between 1985 and 2012. Meanwhile, the U.S. labor force has grown by almost 34 percent during the same period of time. The spike in funding in the last half of the 1990s shown in Table 4.1 was primarily allocated to youth programs such as JobCorps—a program that provides general job-readiness skills and education planning for teens at risk of falling out of the job market.

TABLE 4.1 | FEDERAL WORKFORCE TRAINING FUNDING VS. LABOR FORCE GROWTH, 1979–2012

Fiscal Year	Fed. Appropriation $ in Billions	$ Adjusted for Inflation	% Change Yr. over Yr.	Labor Force (in Millions)	% Growth
1979	10.3	28.9	--	106	--
1985	2.944	6.21	-79%	115	+ 8%
1990	2.914	4.95	-20%	126	+10%
1995	2.537	3.74	-24%	132	+ 5%
2000	3.790	4.95	+32%	141	+ 7%
2005	3.167	3.63	-27%	150	+ 6%
2010	3.199	3.29	- 9%	154	+ 3%
2012	2.827	--	-14%	155	--

Source: ResCare Workforce Services

THE VALUE OF WORKFORCE SERVICE CENTERS

ResCare is one of the largest private administrators of career one-stop centers in the U.S. This privately-held company, which we will learn more about in Chapter 7, is also a leading operator of residential health services—an industry that expects to see massive employment growth as the population ages. We talked to Diane Rath, senior vice-president of ResCare Workforce Services, in late 2012 about the changes in their industry and the importance of their services. Her business unit operates hundreds of career centers in more than 20 states and the District of Columbia, making it the largest single supplier of job-related education and employment assistance under federally funded programs such as the Workforce Investment Act and Temporary Assistance for Needy Families.

Rath explained how ResCare Workforce Services assists a dual customer base: the employer and the job seeker. "Small businesses are often the most frustrated because they don't have an HR department. They don't have the tools, time and resources so they are really struggling to find the workers they need to do the job," she said. On the other hand, she explained, the recession created a unique situation for many job seekers. "So many people have never had to look for a job. Helping them understand how to market themselves and what will be required to find their next career can be a major challenge."

Intermediaries such as ResCare are critical to fixing the skills gap, because they provide a bridge between employers' needs and job seekers who often don't know where to turn next. Many small businesses aren't aware that these services exist, so ResCare sends job developers into communities to assess employers' human capital challenges and the types of vacancies they're trying to fill.

"It is the best kept secret because we deliver the services, which are funded under the public workforce system via employer taxes," she said. "We tell small businesses: you've prepaid for this service, so allow us to help you get the value for the investment you have already made."

ResCare can then function as a proxy HR department—advertising for vacancies, hosting job fairs, prescreening applicants, etc. Rath explained that much of fixing the skills gap is a matter of addressing a "communications gap" between the needs of the employers and the expectations of job seekers, which begins with acknowledging that a lot of technical and STEM-related skills can be acquired through two-year community college programs. Rath says this explains why one of the largest groups of students in community colleges are people that already have a bachelor's or higher degree—individuals just missing a tangible skill that will set them apart. Companies need to better connect themselves to these programs and even go so far as to have a stronger presence within the middle-school and high-school system.

Rath added that the decline of America's vocational education system—in which students learn skills such as welding, electrical work, or masonry in high school—is being felt now, but will be much more significant as demographics shift. "We have a problem in that much of the labor in the skilled trades is retiring or nearing retirement. It's not being replaced," she said.

So if workforce service programs offered by the likes of ResCare are intended to operate as a labor force switchboard—connecting employers to workers and workers to appropriate skills—do they work? Government statistics and success rates aren't often released, but past academic research found that such services are particularly beneficial to workers on the margins of the workforce: dislocated workers with little job search experience, and youth at risk of dropping out of the labor force. Moreover, Rath confirmed that most of ResCare's contracts are paid on performance—which is based on their ability to place unemployed candidates in new roles—as well as measures like wage gains and retention rates. As a private company, ResCare has a huge incentive to meet the needs of job seekers and employers, and in some cases, the company staffs entire organizations through its programs. For example, ResCare, in conjunction with the Texas Workforce Commission and Workforce

Solutions Greater Dallas, organized a job fair that resulted in the recently opened Omni Hotel Dallas hiring hundreds of unemployed job seekers, youths, and recent graduates of skills training programs.

Workforce training services are key to filling in the gaps the education system misses. There will always be dislocated workers and job seekers in need of resources to get them to that next step of their career. But we can't mistake the downward trend in funding, which provides an additional challenge for Rath and her workforce experts. "If you look at the funding today versus funding available twenty years ago, you see that it has been dramatically shrinking at a time when employers are clamoring more than ever for a skilled workforce," she said. "But we still have to meet the needs of our customers either way. We still need to get the word out."

Whether it's through internal training, using workforce training programs offered by organization such as ResCare, or through better integration with community colleges or universities, it is clear employers will have to own more of the process. In the next sections, we show how that's possible.

RE-EMPLOYING THE LONG-TERM UNEMPLOYED

It would be a big mistake to generalize the stories of America's unemployed. Their skills, their education, and their personal histories come in all shades. Here are a few examples.

"My primary work history was working in [the] mortgage documentation business," said Ron Meharg. He helped grow the business, which was eventually acquired by a Fortune 500 company. "Unfortunately we became the victims of the mortgage industry disaster and it put me out of work for a couple of years."

Others, like Sharee Robinson, are transitioning from the full-time responsibility of child-care back to the full-time working world. "I was out of the marketplace because I had children and took five years off," she said. "So I had a really hard time getting a good job that I wanted." Employers just appeared to be skeptical of someone who'd been out of work for so long.

For Chris Wood, a former IT employee who stepped away from the field to pursue his entrepreneurial ambition, the challenge was updating a skill set that hadn't aged well. "I decided to go into business for myself, fulfilling a life-long dream of building a European-style coffee house, which while I was building it, unfortunately, a Starbucks moved in a half-mile down the road," he said. "So I thought about where I was happiest, and it was doing the IT-based work." However, his time away from the profession required that he pick up new training to have a legitimate shot.

Then there are the talented, educated professionals like Ricky Ryles, who jump from opportunity to opportunity, waiting to find something that truly feels right. "I started off in medicine at Emory and worked in kidney transplant as well as eylet cell transplant, which is [a] diabetes research lab," he said. "I decided it wasn't the way I wanted to go. I went into the Air Force; it turned out to be a viable solution for me. I spent six years there and then got another degree in aeronautics." But in a tight market, he still couldn't find a job.

And there are surely millions like Matt Silva, a worker who values his college education, but came to the realization that the job market rewarded expertise in niche areas. "I had a lot of education, but not a lot of technical skills," he said. "I knew that I needed something to become a more viable candidate in the workplace."

Their histories provide a pretty good cross section of the four million-plus long-term unemployed workers in the United States, those who have been out of work for 27 weeks or more: Mature, experienced workers laid off through no fault of their own; parents returning to the workforce to support their family; entrepreneurs whose dreams never fully materialized; skilled veterans attempting to find their niche; and young, college-educated workers missing that one piece keeping them from a truly great job.

But if there's one word that absolutely should not describe any of this group it is "unemployable."

In 2011, CareerBuilder hired all of the job seekers named above, plus five others, as part of a six-month experiment, which was called the "Re-employment Initiative." The project basically functioned like any paid apprenticeship program. The goal was simple: To prove that if companies give unemployed job seekers an opportunity and teach them a skill set, regardless of their past experiences, the individuals will not only succeed a vast majority of the time, but the employers will begin to solve much of their skills gap problem, as well.

But let's take a step back and explain why such initiatives are needed on a mass scale. Any person who wants a job in this country, but can't find one, deserves assistance or an opportunity to grow or develop his or her skills. No one doubts that. But if there's a segment of the unemployed beyond veterans that business leaders and government officials need to target next, it's the long-term unemployed. For each week that passes, members of this group may find themselves closer and closer to dropping out of the labor market altogether, their potential and capacity for productivity wasted. Whether it's a chance to prove themselves when no one thinks they're the right fit for a job opening, or the opportunity to learn a new skill to make their resume more relevant to hiring managers, members of this group need jobs to prevent a massive structural unemployment crisis.

As we pointed out in Chapter 1, as of early 2013, the share of the unemployed population that has been out of work for more than 27 weeks is nearly 40 percent. While that number peaked in 2010 at 45 percent and has been on a slow decline since, this rate is still very high by historical standards. In the years after the 2001 recession, the share of long-term unemployed never got above 24 percent. Before that recession, the share averaged around 11 to 12 percent of the unemployed population. In short, being unemployed today is much different than at any other point in recent memory. Today, there's a four in ten chance an unemployed person will be out of work for six months, one year, or even two or more years. Economists have debated whether or not emergency extensions of unemployment insurance are compounding this trend, but let's say, for the sake of our goal of getting everyone back to work, that most of the long-term unemployed want to reboot their careers as soon as possible.

So why is their job search progressively more difficult as time goes on? In 2011, we asked hiring managers whether or not they were more understanding of employment gaps post-recession. Fortunately, a wide majority said yes (85 percent). But for millions of job seekers, that sentiment hasn't mattered much. Hiring managers said that job seekers with lengthy unemployment gaps could improve their marketability by taking a temp job or trying contract work if their profession is suited to this option. In the surveys, most hiring managers (61 percent) view full-time or part-time volunteer work (which would still allow job seekers to collect benefits) in the same way as they do employment.

Along with taking classes and acquiring new certifications, these suggestions are great things for job seekers to do. But more understanding or not, there's still an overriding sense that hiring managers care quite a bit about employment gaps. In the 2012 CareerBuilder Talent Crunch survey, we found that qualified candidates with no gap in their resume stand a better chance of finding a job than qualified candidates with a large gap in their resume. A slim majority of employers (52 percent) claim they have no preference when faced with a choice between two equally qualified candidates—one unemployed short term, one long term. But for the rest, a major gap exists. Thirty-six percent of employers would choose the person without the lengthy gap, compared to just 11 percent who would bring on the long-term unemployed candidate.

This creates a paradox for the long-term unemployed. If the best chance of getting a job is to find one in your first few months of unemployment, what happens once you cross that threshold? On a policy level, there have been attempts to address this problem by incentivizing the supply side.

In late 2011, the American JOBS (Jump Start Our Business Startups) Act included tax incentives similar to those in the veterans bill that would reward (up to $4,000 per employee) any employer who hired a long-term unemployed candidate. "It makes a lot of sense because what we've seen over the course of the last year or so is [the] folks who are picking up work are the ones who have been unemployed for short periods of time," Ravin Jesuthasan, global head of talent management at Towers Watson, told BenefitsPro.com before the bill was voted on. "Many companies appear to be ignoring the long-term unemployed. Frankly, we're not going to impact any unemployment numbers without an incentive that specifically targets hiring from this pool."[10]

The incentives, which were part of a much larger, $450 billion stimulus bill, were ultimately defeated. But it should not take a tax benefit for many companies to see the rewards of hiring long-term unemployed candidates. Reskilling workers who've been out of a job for a long time isn't nearly the risk some companies make it out to be. This brings us back to the Re-employment Initiative.

Members of CareerBuilder's business intelligence (BI) team, based in the Atlanta area, wanted to find out for themselves whether training unemployed workers could be done successfully. The Re-employment Initiative was definitely an instance of "putting your money where your mouth is." The company intuitively felt that, if given a chance, most ambitious people would flourish when given a new skill. The company's career advisers and spokespeople had preached this belief to media. Visitors to CareerBuilder's website and followers of the company blog told us time and time again, "Why aren't companies more involved in reskilling?" So the BI team decided to take the challenge.

"The Re-employment Initiative is a program we created to give back to the community," said Rob Wittes, a senior business intelligence manager for CareerBuilder. "What we're trying to do is retrain people in specific IT skills that will prepare them for jobs available in the marketplace." Daniel Cosey, senior director of information management for CareerBuilder, notes that the program illustrates how, by acquiring a single new technical skill, workers can exponentially increase their marketability. "Employers struggle to find niche skill sets, but they often underestimate the ability of workers to learn and adapt quickly," he said. "What we want to do is take people of diverse backgrounds, give them a marketable skill, and prove to them and other companies that training is often a quick, viable option to fill in a skills mismatch."

Thus, the goal of the program was not for CareerBuilder to hire the people it trained. Wittes, Cosey, and the other program administrators could have hired the participants after their training period was complete and proclaim success, but that wouldn't prove to anyone that the participants' new skills would make them more competitive in the job market. Would adding in-demand skills be the difference for these people? On paper, it made sense. The hypothesis established was essentially the following: a) The candidates could be trained at a low cost, despite their background or lack of background in IT; b) It could be done without placing a heavy burden on the existing employees doing the mentoring/ training of the program's participants; and, c) The majority of the participants who completed the program would be hired externally shortly after the six-month program's conclusion.

Participants primarily learned Structured Query Language (SQL) and various extensions of SQL—a programming language used for managing data in relational database management systems (RDBMS). In short, it's a crucial BI function in the big data era. SQL is a fixture of software offered by Oracle, Microsoft, and Sybase, among others. Database administrators with SQL skills make a median of $90,000 annually, according to CareerBuilder's Talent Compensation Portal. From 2010–2012, there were anywhere between 2,500 and 5,000 online listings per month seeking workers with SQL proficiency. It's a marketable, in-demand skill.

After their initial training, participants began performing tasks for real-world business clients, so it certainly wasn't like the BI team was getting zero returns from the new hires. By the completion of the six-month term, the participants were working independently and ready for full-time, permanent work.

"I found my passion for data and business intelligence," said Meharg shortly after leaving CareerBuilder. "I had more responses after putting my resume in the last month I've been searching for a job than the entire year and half prior to that."

Soon after, we learned that Meharg took a BI job at Genesis10—a fast-growing business consulting and technology staffing firm. After being unemployed for five years, Sharee Robinson was hired for a permanent position at Primedia as a SQL reporting analyst. Chris Wood was hired as a reporting analyst on a contract-to-hire basis for an accounting and consulting firm. Ricky Ryles used his experience to help in the nonprofit sector (an area desperately in need of skilled tech professionals) and went on to finish an MBA program. Matt Silva is a Crystal Reports developer for RouteMatch, a transportation logistics software company based in Atlanta.

"The way I had been feeling prior [to the program] was that I just needed somebody to give me a chance to prove my worth," Silva said.

For many organizations, starting a training program or apprenticeship defies feasibility. But if all or most companies are unwilling to depart from the status quo, and no one provides training, the available talent pool will continue to shrink and the skills shortage will compound. Understandably, many employers are afraid of trainee flight. However, as we discussed earlier in this chapter, that runs counter to the fact that training opportunities often lead to greater employee engagement and may actually reduce their willingness to leave.

The truth is, however, that programs like this would have to be replicated everywhere around the country to make significant headway. While many large companies significantly invest in training programs, it's clear others do not. Some companies can't afford to be at full staff, let alone hire a handful of paid apprentices or interns and train them. That's understandable. But at a certain point we have to consider alternatives. Companies that do have the capacity to train new hires need to measure the downside to not doing so. Extended vacancies come at a severe cost. So if you're not able to fill a key position within your organization, are unable to recruit talent away from a competitor, or can't find the perfect fit in a new graduate pool, is waiting worth the cost, when in just a short period of time an eager candidate can learn the required skills?

WHEN EMPLOYERS EMPOWER EMPLOYMENT

The good news is that many employers are doing their part. The following examples showcase the multitude of ways companies and communities empower employment—from clearly defined certification and training programs, to examples of hiring for potential.

▶ The story of Wegmans, the popular, privately-owned East Coast supermarket chain that employs more than 40,000 people, provides a link between extensive new-hire training and strong retention. Consistently a mainstay at the top of *Fortune's* Best Places to Work list, Wegmans trains new hires for forty hours before they ever see a customer and, throughout their tenure, associates are given opportunities to hone their expertise. Hundreds of employees each year are flown around the world to learn more about the origins of their products. According to reporter David Rhode, the company has half the turnover of its competitors.[11]

▸ Starbucks seeded $5 million and sponsors customer
donation drives in support of Opportunity Finance Network
(OFN)—a national network of community development
financial organizations that provide affordable, low-risk
lending to small businesses. The recession made it extremely
difficult for many entrepreneurs to gain access to credit
that would inevitably lead to job creation. Note that the
two million-plus small businesses in the U.S. represent
about 45 percent of all employment. Through fiscal year
2011, the 200 members of OFN invested $30 billion
spread across approximately 83,000 businesses, primarily in
urban and underserved areas. Funds also financed housing
developments and community facilities.[12]

▸ Combating skills shortages in information technology
can be a different beast altogether. Skills evolve so fast,
certification giants like Cisco are constantly updating
training procedures. The company, which made its name in
network administration, awards hundreds of thousands of
IT certifications a year—from entry-level to expert—for its
proprietary technologies. Two new programs focus on the
skills gap faced in company data centers, which account for
one of the fastest growing areas in IT. Moreover, the data
center certifications are skills specific and not exclusive to
Cisco products.[13]

As noted by representatives from AT&T in Chapter 2,
addressing future skills needs to begin before students
ever get to college. For instance, only 20,000 high-school
students take the Advanced Placement test for computer
science. Seeing that our economy will likely be dominated by
knowledge workers or tech workers, whom we will rely on to
establish the job-creating companies of the next generations,

the number of young people interested in computer science and related fields is simply not high enough to inspire much confidence. The problem is not going unnoticed, however. Google has awarded nearly $9 million in college scholarships to nearly 2,100 people worldwide. Through the Anita Borg Memorial Scholarship, Google also invites dozens of female award winners to its campus each year for a retreat and seminar intended to increase the number of women in the computer science field.

▸ Similarly, venture capitalists in New York City created the Academy for Software Engineering, a high school in the city's Union Square neighborhood established in 2012. The school will not only address the need for more tech workers, but provide a model of how computer science education can potentially operate nationally.[14] Still though, most school districts will be unable to afford the infrastructure to implement great computer science curricula—let alone find many computer scientists willing to teach full-time when they could just as easily be making double or triple the offered salary elsewhere. For this reason, a Microsoft engineer, Kevin Wang, started Technology Education and Literacy in Schools (TEALS), which allows working computer science professionals to volunteer as adjunct teachers in high schools, while simultaneously training an in-class teacher who will be able to independently instruct within a few semesters.[15] The classes are often taught remotely, allowing TEALS to reach regions otherwise underserved in computer science. In 2012–2013, the program reached more than 2,000 students in 37 schools.

▸ In 2011, Sir Richard Branson, founder and chairman of Virgin Group, encouraged his managing directors worldwide to start hiring more ex-offenders. Recidivism rates among people with a criminal record are so high in part because many face few, if any, economic opportunities after serving time. In the U.S., employers are prohibited from establishing across-the-board bans on hiring offenders, but there's an overwhelming sense that many companies are hesitant to even consider interviewing someone with a criminal record. A recent CareerBuilder survey found that nearly half of U.S. employers do not hire ex-offenders. Branson was inspired after meeting representatives from an Australian transportation company that hired 460 ex-prisoners, none of whom reportedly have committed another crime. Writing in his blog, Branson said, "Research has shown that most ex-offenders are more committed and willing to do more than just the job. They are grateful for the opportunity to do something worthwhile rather than falling back on their former ways and circumstances … Maybe a good employer and the positive influence of work colleagues can, in part, be a replacement for a dysfunctional family."[16]

▶ The Bank of America Foundation has donated more than $22 million in workforce development grants, including financial backing of New Door—a San Francisco-based nonprofit helping at-risk youth prepare for the job market. The organization partners with several area businesses and operates two small businesses of its own: a screen-printing shop and a bicycle sales and repair shop. The small businesses employ New Door's youth participants, teaching them tangible skills and management experience. Bank of America is seeing clear results. In 2010, 100 percent of New Door's previously homeless participants "maintained stable housing during the length of the program and

86 percent went on to new jobs or higher education after job internships."[17]

▸ Penn United Technologies—a high-precision metal manufacturer—recognized that the stagnation of vocational education programs was leading to a shortage of the skills the company and its clients needed. As a result, they adopted a training and apprenticeship model more reminiscent of the German manufacturing sector than the United States'. In 1999, the company built the Learning Institute for Growth of High Technology (L.I.G.H.T.)—a 17,000 square foot training facility for its clients in need of skilled manufacturers as well as its own internal apprenticeship workers. Jim Ferguson, former director of training at L.I.G.H.T., told us that Penn trains anywhere from 20 to 50 of its own apprentices per year, depending on demand. "We knew we had to provide the best learning facility to produce the best people," he said. Ferguson's view is one many industry commentators wish were more commonplace. "If we are going to train the new manufacturing workers to do advanced troubleshooting and have the multi-skill ability to do many jobs as a generalist, I believe it will require long-term, comprehensive training programs," wrote industry expert Mike Collins, in a piece for Manufacturing.net. Collins is not optimistic that companies will follow the lead of Penn United. "I suspect that the publicly held companies will continue to view training as an expense rather than an investment. This kind of mindset is very suspicious of training programs that take years to complete, paying people for skills they attain, or issuing certificates to people that make their skills transferable."[18]

The companies focused on the reskilling of the workforce often take the long view. While certain investments pay off immediately, many of the above stories and initiatives are about laying the foundation for a more capable workforce years down the line. If every medium and enterprise organization could reskill even one worker, we could take a significant step toward tackling present and future skill shortages.

CHAPTER

5

A Better Candidate Experience

"Recruitment, at its core, is marketing," said Gordon Frutiger, director of strategic recruitment initiatives at AIG (American International Group), when we spoke to him in 2012. "I think where companies really struggle is that they attempt to equate their business or consumer brand with their recruitment brand, but they, and even most talent acquisition professionals, have been slow to grasp that the two are distinctly different."

Undoubtedly, when you're involved in leading the recruitment initiatives of a 65,000-plus workforce like Frutiger is, you understand the importance of cultivating an identity for your organization as a place to work. Simply put, a recruitment or employment brand defines the culture of an organization, giving candidates an impression of what it would be like to work there. If you're familiar at all with HR trends of the past few years, you've likely heard the employment branding topic come up countless times in conversation, trade publications, and the HR blogosphere. But even after years in the spotlight, most people involved with the hiring process claim they don't think their companies have an employment brand or aren't sure they have a definable employment brand—that includes 74 percent of hiring managers and 48 percent of HR managers, according to a 2011 CareerBuilder survey. However, everyone has an employment brand whether they know it or not. Employers and workers contribute to its creation, as do the job seekers who receive the recruitment content and form perceptions of a company.

For Frutiger and AIG, a major part of the branding process occurs long before a prospective employee's first talk with a recruiter or sit-down interview. For many candidates, it starts with the job application itself. This is why one of Frutiger's major initiatives is to ensure any candidate can visit the AIG jobs page, read a description, apply for a position, and receive confirmation of that application all within a 10-minute window. This runs counter to most job seekers' experiences. Getting your name on an employer's radar can often be a highly frustrating, time consuming process. That's a problem that multiplies when the job seeker realizes she may have to navigate a different set of clunky application software and employer requirements for each listing. Remarkably, some application systems timeout job seekers if they don't make it through the questions after a certain period of time, forcing them to start over, or more likely, compel them to never seek employment with that firm again.

Frutiger noted that for the talent acquisition function to evolve, all existing traditions must be thrown under the microscope, including the time-honored resume. "When you don't think about a job from the candidate's perspective, you tend to fall into the 'same old, same old.' It's why we still insist on seeing a resume when in fact the resume format as we use it today originated right after WWII," he said. "Think about all that has changed in our world since then, yet the resume remains the same."

Outdated application processes are at the heart of what's wrong with the job search and can severely put a dent in how potentially desirable candidates perceive a company.

Since 2008, CareerBuilder has tracked the experience of more than five million online job seekers, identifying what prompted them to apply for a specific job, and again four weeks later, how they'd rate their communication with the employers. The research also asked candidates who looked at a specific job listing, started the application, and ultimately didn't submit, why they backed out. Nearly one in four job seekers said their dropoff was due to an application that was too long, too confusing, timed them out, or asked for personal information they weren't comfortable sharing at that stage of the process. In all, one-third of all candidates who attempt to apply for a job don't complete the process due to a frustrating experience.

Think about what that means for highly skilled candidates and the organizations trying to lure them. If someone already receiving multiple offers encounters a system that gives even the hint of being an encumbrance, she's going to move on. Respecting candidates' time may seem like an optional behavior in a weak labor market, but data suggests it's necessary. Certainly that's the case if you're going after top talent.

This chapter is about ways companies are improving the recruitment process on both the candidate and employer side of the talent equation. Such improvements begin when the employer researches what motivates their ideal candidate and integrates those triggers with clear messaging in a variety of media. It's difficult to attract quality talent without fine-tuning the employment brand. Once the candidates are hooked, the focus shifts to their experience interacting with the employer directly in the application and interview stages. So while branding and candidate experience are technically different, it's hard to talk about one without touching on the other. We'll interweave both stories, using the opinions and feedback of more than two million job seekers gathered over the past several years. Finally, because a strong culture and workplace identity are key to maintaining an effective workforce, employment branding will be covered in further detail in Chapter 7.

In this chapter we'll cover four areas in the candidate experience space:

▶ First, we'll discuss how candidate experience can affect the bottom line.

▶ Second, we'll describe the basics of building an employment brand.

▸ Third, we'll explore applicant experience at the national level in a survey of more than two million job seekers, connecting it to the difficulty many people have looking for work in the post-recession economy.

▸ Finally, we use the applicant experience data to illustrate how one health care company stacks up against industry competitors.

NEGATIVE CANDIDATE EXPERIENCE CAN AFFECT BOTTOM LINE

We're not suggesting in this chapter that companies receiving millions of applications annually deserve a scolding for failing to satisfy every interested job seeker. There is ultimately going to be a significant contingency of disappointed people. It's the reality of the recruitment process. And certainly no one's suggesting recruiters mail personal thank you letters. That's a straw man argument. It's as impossible as it is impractical. Another challenge in the candidate experience space is the justifiable policy of not responding to rejected candidates until the position is filled. An interview process will often break down, requiring the hiring manager to go back to the 'maybe' pile. On the other hand, the typical job seeker wants to know their status within days, but the position may not be filled for weeks or months. By the time the selected candidate signs the offer letter, the job seekers who weren't granted an interview have likely long given up hope of being called back.

But technology enables fairly simple solutions that would eliminate much of the ill will. Perhaps the most commonly used tactic is the "don't call us, we'll call you" e-mail. It goes something like this: "Thank you for your interest in Company XYZ. Due to the large volume of interested candidates, we'll only notify you if you are deemed a fit for the position." This is an efficient approach to acknowledging receipt, but isn't aimed at improving candidate care. For one, it primarily serves to dampen job seeker expectations. It is code for: good luck because you're going to need it.

Frutiger's other major initiative at AIG is the creation of an opt-in text message notification system for applicants. When the status of the job changes, the candidate will be notified immediately. For example, when a recruiter reviews your resume, when the hiring manager requests the interview, when the job is filled, or when they've decided to make you an offer, you'll receive a text. This is very much the automation of personalization, which sounds like an oxymoron, but actually ensures individuals are on the same page as the employer. It also ensures a status change won't get lost in the candidate's e-mail inbox.

But as the applicant volume increases, courtesy begins to cost money. So what's the value proposition of keeping candidates in the loop? The bar graphs shown in Figure 5.1 represent the behavior of satisfied and dissatisfied job seekers.

FIGURE 5.1 | POST-APPLICATION BEHAVIOR OF SATISFIED AND DISSATISFIED JOB APPLICANTS

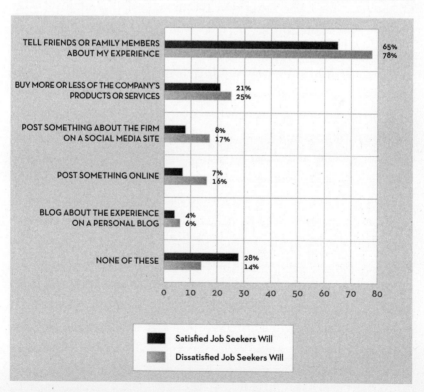

Source: CareerBuilder/Inavero Job Seeker Path Study, 2011

For some large consumer companies, this data is hardly insignificant. When one in four ignored candidates chooses to buy less of a company's products or services, it can amount to millions in lost revenue and thousands of lost customers annually. It also speaks to the reality that negative experiences are far more likely to go viral than a positive story.

To address these potential pitfalls, Frutiger and AIG are attempting to do away with any flaws in their system. In the case of time spent applying, Frutiger challenged his recruiting leaders to scale back the process to something a bit greater than a simple name and e-mail form and a task significantly less cumbersome than copy and pasting fifteen years of work history in individual chunks. This may mean AIG ultimately simplifies or skips the resume upload, integrates social media or online professional profiles, or uses brief video recordings utilizing candidates' webcams. As long as the entire process can be completed in under 10 minutes, they're likely to explore the idea.

But what about hiring managers who see application length as a way to weed out people not qualified or not serious about the position? The logic held by proponents of this camp suggests that a ten-page application, in which applicants are asked to type in answers to questions already addressed in resumes or cover letters, is a test to determine *who is really interested in the job*. While it's true a short application could attract more unqualified candidates, it enhances the applicant pool by appealing to skilled workers who don't feel they should have to jump through hoops to apply for a position. Frutiger noted that for skilled positions, companies need to attract all potential candidates, including full-time workers who are only semi-active in their job search. "By making this group go through a false kind of test, aren't you ruling out a good 70 percent of the labor market?" he said, noting that hiring managers and recruiters need to put themselves in a candidate's shoes. "If you think of yourself as quality talent, then why are you asking someone to do something you would never do? Too many companies and too many talent acquisition groups unfortunately put the burden on the candidate." Frutiger's point is magnified by the fact that seven in ten full-time workers frequently browse new job opportunities and three in ten do so as part of their regular routine, according to a 2012 Career-Builder survey.

The 10-minute application initiative falls under the umbrella of AIG's broader effort to put the candidate first in the talent acquisition process. Every AIG recruiter works off a peer-created candidate care guide that establishes the mission of their prospect-centered process. Its mission statement is simple:

> "AIG believes a thoughtful customer-focused approach that carefully manages the candidate's experience, builds our brand as a great place to work and delivers results. We strengthen our relationships with prospects and clients, converting more resumes into candidates and more candidates into accepted offers and more new hires who believe they've made the right choice to join our company."

The open communication is extended directly to the job seeker. Before candidates sit down for an interview, they're given a simple card that defines how AIG intends to treat them for the rest of the process:

▸ We will clearly define our job profiles so you can better determine which opportunities match your career goals.

▸ We will respect your time with us, sharing interview details with you in advance and adhering to schedules as much as possible.

▸ We will provide you with helpful information about the role, the team, and the department in advance of the interview to help you prepare and perform well in the interview.

▸ Any meeting you come to will be a dialogue, giving you the chance to get answers to your questions.

▸ We will aim to provide interview feedback.

Frutiger says candidates are told up front that they're free to call out AIG if at any point they fail on one of these promises.

AIG's philosophy is unique in the sense that it comes at a time when employers believe they hold all the cards in the hiring game. There's relatively low demand for labor but a high supply of potential employees. With so many people in the mix—qualified or not—the hiring manager or recruiter could easily adopt a mindset of: "The only candidate that matters is the one I ultimately hire." There are two problems with that logic. First, the best candidates will apply in greater numbers to an employer that communicates more strongly. Secondly, all those other candidates you ignored or put off may be customers or future customers, or they may share their experience with other potential customers via social media.

The latter point reinforces the close link between the corporate/consumer brand and the employer brand; while distinct, one can easily influence the other. Frutiger noted the significance of the company's positive turnaround since the financial crisis, specifically the fact that the federal government no longer holds a stake in the firm after it owned 92 percent of shares at one point in 2011. AIG is not shy about their role in the financial crisis when interacting with job candidates. A video prominently featured on their career page during 2012 and embedded within their online postings stated plainly: "Perhaps no other company came to represent that crisis more than AIG." The video goes on to explain AIG's 2010 promise to repay the U.S. government and American taxpayers in full with a profit, while at the same time becoming smaller and more focused through restructuring. It was a promise they kept. However, Frutiger said this business story isn't as important to a prospective candidate as telling the story of the job itself. The most important challenge in conveying an employment brand and kicking off the applicant's experience correctly is to clearly illustrate what the candidate would be doing on the job if she were to get it. A processed PR message or a five-paragraph job description will not resonate nearly as well as an actual AIG employee explaining via video what the day-to-day job is like and what it requires—a tactic Frutiger intends to move toward employing for many of his listings.

THE FOUNDATION OF THE EMPLOYMENT BRAND

In order to tell your story effectively, you need to understand when the job seeker truly begins engaging with your brand. What are the first steps of the job search process? According to a survey of both active and passive job seekers conducted by CareerBuilder and Inavero in 2011, stage one is an internally focused evaluation of the individual's personal networks and the companies for which they'd most like to work (see Figure 5.2). Note that this stage does not involve a broad, open-ended job search.

What this suggests is that the companies first targeted by a job seeker will be ones they already have in their head as ideal employers or are companies their professional networks recommend. From an employment branding perspective, the job search technically begins long before candidates actually begin searching for jobs. Most of us are always consciously or unconsciously developing perceptions of organizations via professional or consumer interactions; when it

FIGURE 5.2 | TOP FIVE BEHAVIORS ONCE THE SEARCH BEGINS

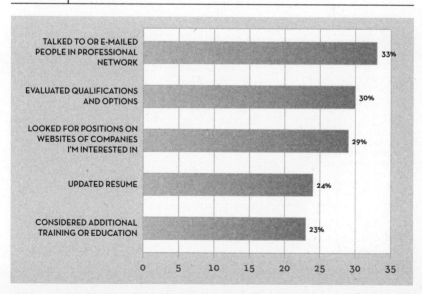

Source: CareerBuilder/Inavero Job Seeker Path Study, 2011

FIGURE 5.3 | RESOURCES USED BY ACTIVE JOB SEEKERS

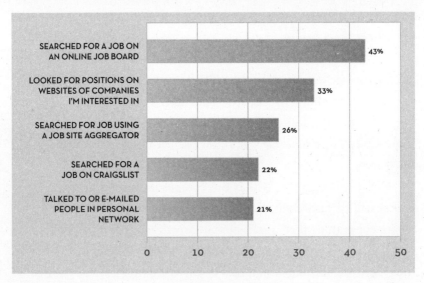

Source: CareerBuilder/Inavero Job Seeker Path Study, 2011

comes time to evaluate these organizations as potential employers, those previously formed opinions come into play.

This naturally gives the advantage to larger companies or publicly-known brands. However, most job seekers widen the playing field as they move their search forward, as shown in Figure 5.3. Each visit to a company page or online job listing is an opportunity to make an impression on prospective candidates.

A 2012 CareerBuilder candidate behavior survey found that the average worker uses 15 sources when searching for a job—more sources than are used for researching new insurance providers, banks, or vacations. Job seekers (whether they are working full-time and exploring greener pastures or are unemployed) are voracious seekers of information. This means companies must be strategic and thorough in how they disseminate their employment brands. The list provided in the sidebar and published in the CareerBuilder "Start Branding" e-book features five of the most common mechanisms to communicate employment brands.

Five Resources for Communicating an Employment Brand

1. **Job Advertisements**: Job ads are often the first introduction job seekers have to your company, so make them count. In addition to offering a clear description of the job roles and responsibilities, take the opportunity to discuss the company, its mission, values, and goals, as well as benefits you offer and any recognition your company has received for its employment practices.

2. **Your Company's Career Center**: As one of the most important outlets for disseminating your brand message, your career site should be easily navigable and clearly communicate what it's like to work at the company. Be creative in how you illustrate your company by utilizing employee testimonials, "day in the life" videos, or highlighted "job of the month" opportunities, for example.

3. **Your Employees**: Employee referral programs are another effective way to communicate your company's employment brand, while at the same time identifying job candidates. Often, the best way to recruit qualified employees is through word of mouth, and satisfied employees are the best messengers. Research demonstrates that word of mouth is perceived as at least twice as credible as advertisements. Leveraging employees obviously necessitates that they first understand and buy into the employment brand (and that you treat them well).

4. **Local or National Media**: Sending out press releases or applying for "best places to work" competitions can help your company gain recognition and publicity from credible third-party organizations, further spreading your company's brand message and broadening your exposure.

5. **Social Media**: One of the newest—and still developing— avenues for communicating your brand, social media has become a critical component of today's recruitment strategy.[1]

At the end of the day, much of the employment brand is developed as a consequence of an organization's actions rather than its marketing. "While it is still possible to heavily influence perception with well-managed efforts, significant growth in social media, peer-to-peer content publishing, and online rating services have shifted a majority of the power away from the corporate employer brand manager to the masses," said Dr. John Sullivan, an HR guru writing for the website ERE.net. "Their points of view are often emotionally charged, personal, and therefore, significantly more trusted as fact by those you need to influence."[2] In other words, a good reputation is earned in the social media era. Companies that treat job candidates well—no different than their clients and consumers—are much more likely to immunize themselves from the negative side of Internet word of mouth. These companies will organically grow their employer brand and attract higher quality candidates.

MEASURING APPLICANT EXPERIENCE

To better understand the potential of big data in the applicant experience process, let's walk through the results of the nationwide CareerBuilder study referenced at the beginning of this chapter. The Applicant Experience Study collected the opinions of approximately two million job seekers between January 2009 and April 2012. In this section, we'll first explore how job seekers analyze the job description itself and proceed to their experience communicating with the company and its recruiters. The power of this data allows companies to judge their own results next to industry benchmarks, as we'll see through a case study later in the chapter.

WHY DO OUR CANDIDATES APPLY?

What we know from Gordon Frutiger and others like him is that the candidates' experience begins well before they submit a cover letter and resume. The job posting itself can influence the quality and number of candidates that apply. So before a company haphazardly revamps their employer branding or decides it's best to emphasize the company bonus structure in the first paragraph of the listing, it's necessary to at least ask "Why are our candidates applying in the first place?"

Figure 5.4 looks at two date ranges. The first is from the early part of the recovery and the second captures job seekers' views from 2011 and 2012.

FIGURE 5.4 | TOP REASONS FOR APPLYING TO A COMPANY

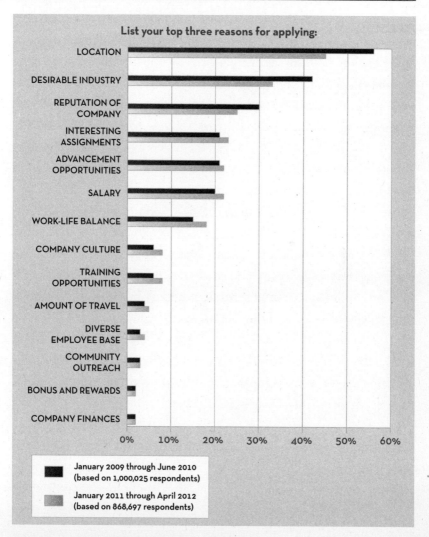

Source: CareerBuilder Applicant Experience Survey

Here are the important takeaways:

The map matters. Location trumps all reasons for applying by a long shot—regardless of the industry. It's foreseeable in the near future that physical offices will become less and less prevalent in the white collar world, but for now, work is still very much geographical. The location of a job dictates the type of applicant pool an organization will get more than any single factor. The reasons for this are innumerable: rising transportation costs, mental health/family benefits of living near work, relocation costs, etc. This was especially true in 2009 and 2010. Workforce mobility at the beginning of the recovery hit an all-time low, largely due to the housing crisis. Many underwater homeowners were unable to leave town for a better opportunity, even if they found one. This hurt employers needing to import high-skill talent and job seekers stuck in particularly hard-hit local economies. However, the number of job applicants that said location was among the top results plummeted by eleven points in 2011 and 2012. This could run parallel to positive signals in the housing market or reflect a growing urgency of the long-term unemployed deciding to widen their acceptable boundaries of employment.

In terms of applicant experience, there's not a whole lot most talent acquisition leaders can do to counteract this structural issue. But if location continues to restrict access to necessary talent pools, executives should explore telecommuting options or relocation packages to attract high-value workers. As we'll see in Chapter 6, just because a skills gap is local does not infer that it's global. Predictive supply and demand is changing the way some companies recruit nationally, and on some levels, dictates where or when businesses will open.

Sell the organization's name and the job assignment. Out-of-work job seekers are often willing to do any job, regardless of the company or industry. But even though the percentage of applicants who selected a desirable industry or reputation of company as one of their top three reasons to apply fell in recent years, an organization's identity remains the backbone of recruitment marketing. Frankly, "a job is just a job," is not a belief many people subscribe to. It's no coincidence "What do you do?" is the first question you'll get after being introduced to someone. To start a new job is to add a new layer to your identity. At some point in the process—be it the first time you read the job description or the moment you decide whether to accept an offer—the question of "Is this an employer I can be happy working for?" will cross your mind. As Figure 5.4 indicates, 25 percent of job seekers chose a company's reputation as a top reason for applying in the more recent date range. If an organization were to individually score significantly higher than the 25 percent benchmark, it's a sign their employer brand is successfully defined.

But the work itself is equally important. "Interesting assignments" piques peoples' interest, because doing work you've never done before or in a way you've never done it, can ignite a feeling of excitement at the point of application. It boils down to a simple proposition: Do I want to apply for this job or do I want to apply for a position that is truly something new? If you want the best candidate pool possible, a job posting that falls in the latter category is going to bring you your desired applicants much faster than copying and pasting the standard job description.

Opportunity versus salary. In both the 2009 and 2011 surveys, salary came in at sixth in the ranking. In part, this has to do with the fact that not all job posts include an estimated salary range. It can't be in one's top three reasons for applying if it's not there. But even so, salary expectations are relatively fixed when you begin a job search; meaning, you know based on your industry and experience level roughly what you should expect. Negotiating pay is something that comes later in the process. What can differentiate job listings is instilling a sense that a candidate will find a job that offers either security or is laden with opportunity. A company that tells entry-level applicants their contributions can lead to broader opportunities is going to beat the company that posts a base salary and calls it a day. Both are extrinsic motivators, but emphasizing opportunity speaks to the national psyche in the post-recession era.

The crisis rattled people's sense of security. Long-tenured employees lost their jobs and college graduates struggle to get their feet wet in their areas of expertise. Thus, job seekers are drawn to positions that sincerely offer an environment of stability and security. Advertising career paths and advancement opportunities is just as important a motivator as the pay itself.

Work–life balance and skills training win Millennials. Most reasons for applying were consistent across generations; however, Millennials (ages 18 to 29) differ from experienced professionals (46 and older) in a few areas. Twenty-one percent of younger workers chose work–life balance among their top three reasons for applying, compared to 17 percent of experienced workers. Development opportunities also are more appealing to young professionals; 14 percent of Millennials selected training opportunities as a top reason, compared to just 8 percent of experienced workers. The inverse is true of a company's reputation. Twenty-six percent of experienced workers are much more likely to cite reputation as a top reason for applying, compared to 18 percent of younger workers. These factors are important across segments, but Millennials look more to flexible workplaces and learning environments, while older generations are more likely to be drawn to brand prestige.

THE BLACK HOLE

Let's continue our discussion of candidate experience and employment branding by discussing one of the biggest challenges confronting job seekers and employers alike. It's been dubbed in the media as the "black hole." Candidates browse, upload, and apply en masse—oftentimes for jobs they're amply qualified to hold—but that's as far as the process goes for some of them. What happened? Where did the resume go? Some are unanswered after days, weeks, or even months. In fact, 75 percent of workers who applied to jobs in 2012 using varying resources never heard back from at least one employer, according to a CareerBuilder job search survey. As a result, many job seekers consider it a victory to just hear back personally from an employer in a timely fashion.

While it is true most positions are filled internally or by a candidate who was directly referred to the role, job boards and other online sources provide 86 percent of external hires, according to a 2012 study by HR technology firm SilkRoad.[3] If that's the case, why do seemingly good resumes go missing? In most circumstances, human resources managers will tell you it all has to do with volume. The *Wall Street Journal*'s Lauren Weber provided an example of two companies that illustrates the challenge clearly:

"Starbucks Corp. attracted 7.6 million job applicants over the past twelve months for about sixty-five thousand corporate and retail job openings; Proctor & Gamble Inc. got nearly a million applications last year for two thousand new positions plus vacant jobs."[4]

Similar stories exist for almost every Fortune 1000 company. Assuming one position attracts five hundred applicants, the initial pool is whittled down to just a handful of people who are invited to interview. But job seekers aren't always familiar with how the five hundred becomes five. In an ideal world, HR departments would have the resources to scour each application with care and hands-on discernment. However, the cost of filling one open position is fairly high as it is. A 2011 Bersin & Associate report found that the average cost per hire is $3,479—a figure that goes up even further for midsize and small businesses.[5] In a labor market flowing with eager job candidates, cost per hire would soar without technology-based recruitment tools to carry at least some of the burden.

The most common tool used is the applicant tracking system (ATS). In most cases, recruiters use an ATS to collect resumes and screen the initial high volume batch. The goal of a well-designed ATS is to weed out resumes that don't meet the minimum qualifications as laid out by the employer. This leaves the recruiter or hiring manager with a more manageable and, ideally, higher-quality pool of talent from which to choose. Although the technology has improved immensely in recent years, it still leaves many job seekers feeling like they're trying to beat a computer rather than applying for a job. This has resulted in countless job seeker advice articles on how to survive the screening process by using key words from the job listing or formatting the resume appropriately. The frustration isn't entirely unwarranted. Companies often establish overly restrictive parameters or "knock-out" questions that eliminate qualified candidates before human eyes ever get to evaluate their profile. It's in an organization's best interest to fine tune what information can successfully be judged by a computer and what is best left to the subjectivity of the human eye.

But if used appropriately, these systems allow already scaled-back HR departments to focus more of their energy toward interacting with candidates, while reducing cost per hire. When the labor market fully recovers, this notion of the black hole should dissipate as the ratio between applicants and vacancies shrinks to prerecession levels. In the meantime, employers whose practices propagate the perceived black hole should know that ignoring the candidate's experience could hurt the bottom line on the consumer end. The point is that the black hole and other distressing metaphors characterizing the contemporary job search process illustrate the importance of acknowledging and caring for the job candidate's experience. Technology can either be a boon or a hindrance in improving a job seeker's perception. It's also one area that big data can be used to both identify problems in the process and point to solutions.

First, though, it's critical to understand that much of the candidate's experience in the application process is primed by the first impression.

Employer Communication Post-Application

So now they've applied. Some may have spent seconds uploading a stock resume; others may have spent hours editing and writing the concise, game-changing cover letter. They might have spent a half hour alone just filling out form after form in an online application. Now they wait to see if their application gets traction. It's an anxious feeling millions go through every day. They need a job, they found your company to be an ideal employer, and they're fairly confident they're a right fit for you. For whatever reason, you sold them. Think of this as any other consumer transaction. You hooked them with marketing, now what do you do when they step foot in your store? Ignore them? Deliver terrible service? Obviously you probably wouldn't be in business if that was the protocol.

Candidate experience is 90 percent communication. So how are companies doing?

The second phase of the study checked back in with applicants a month after initially applying. At this point in time, job seekers were at different stages of the process. Many hadn't heard back from the employer yet. Some were invited to interview, but had not yet begun the process. Others had already been on at least one interview and were awaiting results. Some had received a rejection notice, and other respondents told us they eliminated the company from consideration for various reasons. No matter the grouping, it's clear *some* type of communication is critical to preserving a positive reputation in the minds of job seekers.

In fact, there's a drastic difference between outright rejecting a candidate and ignoring them completely. Almost one in five job seekers has a better impression of the company even after being rejected. That's a benchmark worth tracking. Something is being done right when a candidate's interactions leave them without a job, but with a higher appreciation for the organization. Those individuals will be more likely to apply to your company again if the opportunity arises, and even if they'll never be a fit, they remain a potential ambassador of your brand by way of the consumer marketplace.

Applicants who were eliminated for jobs they had applied to provide the following information about their opinion of the company after hearing back:

▶ I have a better opinion of the company: 17 percent

▶ I have a worse opinion of the company: 29 percent

▶ My opinion is unchanged: 54 percent

Compare that to the opinions of applicants who were ignored by companies they applied to:

- ▸ I have a better opinion of the company: 2 percent

- ▸ I have a worse opinion of the company: 44 percent

- ▸ My opinion is unchanged: 54 percent

The gap between receiving a simple e-mail or call—automated or not—and ignoring applicants altogether is a stunning 15 percentage points in both directions. This amounts to millions of Americans who now have worse impressions of companies due to a (preventable) lack of courtesy. The share of those with negative opinions differs by industry, as well. Job seekers in IT or finance are significantly more likely to turn against companies that snub them:

- ▸ IT: 49 percent

- ▸ Finance: 48 percent

- ▸ Sales: 47 percent

- ▸ Retail: 43 percent

- ▸ Health care: 41 percent

Another important finding: timeliness matters. We tracked more than 31,000 job seekers who applied for jobs in 2012. For this analysis, we disregarded what type of response the candidate received, whether it was a request for an interview, recruiter prescreen, or rejection. We only wanted to know how improving or worsening perceptions were affected by the timeliness of any communication with the employer. The results are shown in Figure 5.5.

Applicants who heard back from the company within three days of applying are much more likely to have a better perception of the company (44 percent compared to only 33 percent of applicants who heard back three to four weeks after applying).

FIGURE 5.5 | THE EFFECT OF TIMELINESS ON CANDIDATE PERCEPTIONS

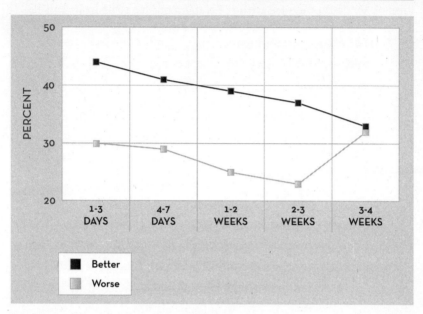

Source: CareerBuilder Applicant Experience Survey, 2012

The same line of thinking does *not* apply to worsening perceptions. In fact, those who hear back between weeks one and three are less likely to have a worse opinion of the employer than at any time before or after. While we can't definitively point to why this is so, it likely has to do with the expectations of the job seeker. For example, let's say two experienced sales managers were laid off during the recession. The first applies to a company and gets a rejection notice the next day. He's fairly disappointed. *Ten years of experience, an hour spent applying, and they reject me outright?* The second gets a rejection 10 days later. She's of course disappointed but doesn't hold it against the employer. *At least they took the time to consider me and notified me within a reasonable time frame.*

However, there's zero chance your employment brand is better off if you skip communicating entirely. A separate 2011 study of unemployed job seekers and full-time workers who were looking for new jobs sums up the state of applicant experience in the post-recession labor market.

Participants were asked to evaluate the following statements and rate the level of which they agreed with the statement on a scale from 1 to 10.

1. My experience during the application process impacts my decision to accept a job or continue searching within the organization.

2. My interaction with companies I have applied to matches what I expected based on their reputations.

3. Companies I have applied to have been responsive during the application process.

Forty percent of respondents rated statement one with a 9 or 10; the statement averaged a 7.1, illustrating the importance of candidate experience. However, the respondents rarely felt those expectations were met. Only 16 percent and 10 percent, respectively, rated the next two statements with a 9 or 10.

There isn't just a need for a better candidate experience. There's an opportunity here, as well. Across the board, companies are failing to impress job seekers with their hiring process. Regardless of whether you feel that's an important consideration, shouldn't the fact that so many companies are neglecting aspiring employees become an opportunity to show yours is the brand that cares more? Moreover, the consequences of failing to live up to your reputation can mean a lot more than hurt feelings.

EXPERIENCE WITH RECRUITERS

Much of candidate experience is influenced by interactions with recruiters. They're often the first human representative with whom the candidate speaks; their knowledge, passion, and sales pitch are as important to the employment brand as the career page. For the most part, according to the applicant experience study, talent acquisition chiefs should be encouraged that, on a national level, recruiters are doing their jobs fairly well. Table 5.1 details the results.

TABLE 5.1 | CANDIDATE PERCEPTIONS OF RECRUITERS

The recruiter was knowledgeable about the job and industry	
Strongly Agree	59%
Somewhat Agree	20%
Neutral	9%
Somewhat Disagree	4%
Strongly Disagree	4%
NA	4%

The recruiter was enthusiastic, represented company as employer of choice	
Strongly Agree	56%
Somewhat Agree	19%
Neutral	13%
Somewhat Disagree	4%
Strongly Disagree	4%
NA	4%

The recruiter was professional in their communication	
Strongly Agree	65%
Somewhat Agree	17%
Neutral	7%
Somewhat Disagree	3%
Strongly Disagree	5%
NA	3%

Source: CareerBuilder Applicant Experience Study, 2012

However, the picture is not all rosy. Most companies will likely strive to be in the 80–90th percentile of recruiter communication. Recruiters are the front-line ambassadors of the employment brand. They not only have to evaluate candidates' interest and aptitude, but

TABLE 5.2 | INTERVIEW CANDIDATES' PERCEPTIONS OF EMPLOYER COMMUNICATIONS

I have a better opinion	37%
I have a worse opinion	18%
My opinion is unchanged	45%

Source: CareerBuilder Applicant Experience Study, 2012

sell candidates on the job and company. Any hedging or perceived inability to answer candidates' questions could cause a drop off in interested talent. This is especially true the higher up the skill ladder you climb.

The study found that a red flag was raised for about a fifth of all candidates invited to interview, as shown in Table 5.2.

Something is happening between the application, recruiter call, and the interview stage. Logic has it that a job seeker should be elated for the opportunity, but it's entirely possible these candidates haven't started their employer research until they get the first call back. And for some, what they're finding isn't all positive. In preparation for the interview, employer research or recruiter communication has turned their opinion of the employer negative. Perhaps it's the discovery that the job itself isn't as promising as the description made it out to be. Perhaps the recruiter gave them an uneasy feeling. Perhaps information about pay, hours, or benefits fell below expectations. Whatever the answer, this is untenable for a successful recruitment strategy. If one-fifth of all selected interviewees have a worse opinion of the employer before they ever meet the hiring manager, the organization is at an increased risk of a bad hire or a prolonged, costly vacancy. Obtaining metrics at every step of the applicant experience process can help companies pinpoint and eliminate hidden trouble spots.

* * *

The preceding discussion provided an overview of applicant experience at the macro level. While it crystallizes the importance of an identifiable employment brand and smooth recruitment process, it doesn't necessarily help individual firms arrive at actionable conclusions. For that discussion we'll turn to an organization that uses their own candidate experience data, benchmarking it against other organizations in the industry.

NEMOURS FOUNDATION: BENCHMARKING APPLICANT EXPERIENCE

Nemours Children's Hospital, located in Orlando, Florida, opened its doors to patients on October 22, 2012. The $397 million, 630,000 square foot facility is state-of-the-art. It includes 95 beds (all in private rooms), a full-service pediatric emergency department, and neonatal and pediatric intensive care units. The hospital was built on a 60-acre campus that includes research and education facilities, as well as a new outpatient clinic. The hospital is owned and operated by the Nemours Foundation, an internationally recognized children's health system that also operates the Nemours/Alfred I. duPont Hospital for Children in Wilmington, Delaware, and more than 30 associated clinics and primary care practices in the Delaware Valley, Florida, Pennsylvania, and New Jersey.

In mid-October, days before the first patients arrived at the new hospital, we chatted with members of the talent acquisition team responsible for staffing the facility, discussing the many successes and challenges of recruiting a team of health practitioners who are equally as impressive as the facility itself.

"We had a huge undertaking before us. We are transitioning from being a one-hospital system with a lot of clinics to a two-hospital system," said Brian Richardson, a physician recruiter in central Florida for Nemours. "We understand that the buildings are great, but it is the people that differentiate institutions. We needed to have all the pieces in place to prepare ourselves for this recruitment task."

In February 2012, Nemours posted several hundred positions on their recruitment website. By the end of August, they had more than 500 critical and frontline positions filled. By the end of 2012, they had filled 620 positions. How did they find the people they needed—many in high-skill or sub-specialized medical fields—while simultaneously preserving a positive candidate experience? To make it happen, Nemours instituted several strategies considered unconventional by some.

The first was the opening of a preview center for candidates, patient families, and the surrounding community. Richardson explained that part of the challenge of attracting the right candidates was that for months there wasn't much to show prospective talent. There is only so much that artist renderings, blueprints, and descriptions of the planned hospital can do to excite prospects about the opportunity. The preview center opened in 2011, and was part information center, part employment office, and part living laboratory for patient room design, furnishings, and technology. Visitors could tour full-scale replicas of an outpatient exam room, emergency room, ICU, and surgical inpatient room. Hiring managers and recruiters used the preview center to conduct high-volume interviewing.

The preview center also represented an extension of the Nemours family-centered brand. It was just as much a site for prospective patients and their families as it was for job candidates—and that was no coincidence. To Nemours, families are partners with doctors, nurses, and all of the organization's associates in the care of their child. Their philosophy is a deliberate step away from authority-driven health care decision making. As a result, patients' and families' interactions with both the personnel and the facility were integral to the hospital's planning. Patient families were invited to serve on the Nemours Family Advisory Council, providing valuable input in the design process—from the floor plan, to the furniture and artwork. They were also carefully trained to interview finalists for leadership and physician positions. The council is made up of local moms and dads, many of whom have children with chronic health conditions, bringing an interesting perspective to the hiring process. The tactic is truly unique, and reinforces the idea to prospective candidates that the family is at the center of every decision made at a Nemours facility. Melissa Beckler, talent acquisition manager at Nemours, explained that the parent interviewers ultimately influenced many hiring managers' decisions.

The recruitment for Nemours Children's Hospital all took place on top of normal day-to-day operations for the modestly-sized HR staff. While the project required the use of contract workers to assist with the substantial additional workload, Beckler's team was enthusiastic and satisfied with the process. In the end, Beckler said her team received more than 97,000 expressions of interest for the 600 jobs ultimately posted for the new hospital and clinic. Considering the workload of the recruiters, we wondered if the candidate experience was compromised; however, the data showed otherwise.

BENCHMARKING APPLICANT EXPERIENCE DATA

Nemours issues to its candidates the same CareerBuilder applicant experience survey questions detailed earlier in this chapter. The data allows the organization's recruiting team to compare their performance to industry benchmarks. It also shows them what attracts job seekers to Nemours. Candidates were provided two surveys by CareerBuilder: The first survey was implemented at the start of the application process; the second was delivered four weeks later, asking candidates about communication during the interim.

The data provides intelligence in a number of areas:

▸ Employment brand

▸ Advertisement effectiveness

▸ Process/technology efficiency

▸ Recruitment team effectiveness

▸ Candidate demographics (who is applying)

Here are some of the key insights from the data.

DOES CANDIDATE EXPERIENCE AFFECT PERCEPTION OF NEMOURS?

The Nemours applicant experience report shows that 40 percent of applicants who were contacted directly by a Nemours representative have a better perception of the organization as a result of that communication. This is slightly above the industry benchmark (39 percent). The data also suggests Nemours's existing reputation is strong. In other words, it's hard to improve upon solid public opinion. So perhaps a better indicator of the positive sentiment is found when we look at the inverse situation shown in Figure 5.6: candidates who said they received no communication from Nemours after applying.

By seven percentage points (39 percent vs. 32 percent) Nemours applicants are more immune to a less-than-ideal application process than applicants to comparable organizations. The overwhelming majority of applicants who did not hear back from a recruiter maintained their positive opinion.

The "word of mouth" test is another way to get an accurate read on candidates' perceptions—in other words, how likely are they to recommend the organization to peers? We took the responses from the graph shown in Figure 5.7 and scored the overall results on a scale from −100 percent to +100 percent, comparing this to industry competitors. Ideally, an organization would have more promoters (+%) than detractors (−%). Figure 5.7 includes candidates who applied but had not been invited to interview, nor had they been denied. The average industry score for health care organizations is +2 percent. Nemours has an impressive +30 percent.

There are two likely explanations for this gap. First, Nemours has a very strong employment brand that excites prospects pre-application.

FIGURE 5.6 | PERCEPTION OF NEMOURS BY CANDIDATES WHO DIDN'T HEAR BACK FROM A RECRUITER

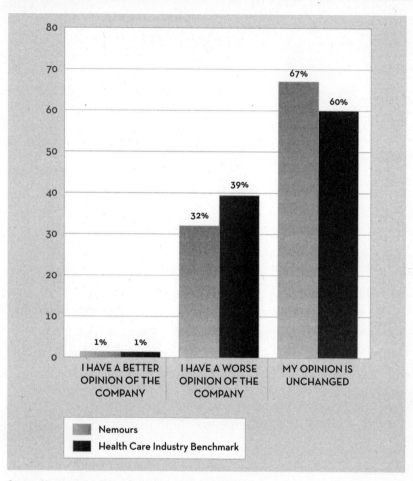

Source: Nemours Applicant Experience Report, 2012

In fact, 54 percent of Nemours applicants cite the "Reputation of the Company" as one of the top three reasons for applying, compared to 22 percent of candidates at other health care organizations. Second, the application itself—the content and the technical process—is simplified as compared to other organizations. Nemours applicants are much more willing to be a brand ambassador even if they're uncertain whether or not they'll be asked for an interview or eventually offered a job. But it's not an

FIGURE 5.7 | APPLICANTS' LIKELIHOOD TO RECOMMEND NEMOURS

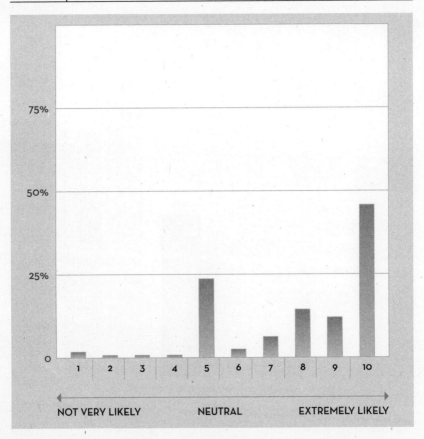

Source: Nemours Applicant Experience Report, 2012

anomaly at this stage alone. Nemours also exceeds benchmarks for candidates who don't finish the application, for candidates invited to interview, and for candidates ultimately not asked to interview.

DOES THE APPLICATION ITSELF MATTER?

Let's test our hypotheses regarding Nemours' above average "perception" marks, starting with the application. The graph shown in Figure 5.8 represents the percentage of job seekers who successfully apply at Nemours as well as those who start but do not finish the application (drop-offs).

FIGURE 5.8 | HAVE YOU APPLIED FOR AN OPPORTUNITY AT NEMOURS IN THE PAST WEEK?

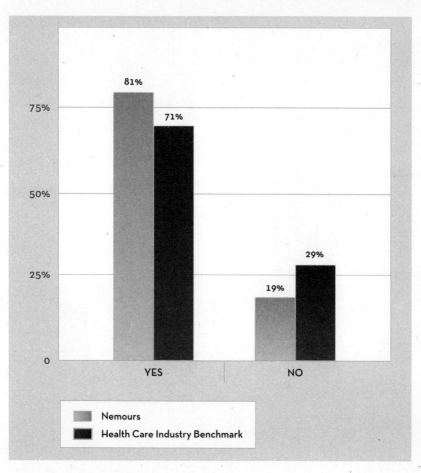

Source: Nemours Applicant Experience Report, 2012

Nemours candidates are more likely to finish applications than candidates at comparable organizations. Why is this so? Based on our conversation with AIG's Frutiger, one of the major reasons high drop-off rates exist is application length. As shown in Figure 5.9, Nemours is ahead of its industry competitors by 12 percentage points in the category "application is shorter than others." Think about why application length is important for health care professionals. Those who are

FIGURE 5.9 | CANDIDATE PERCEPTIONS OF NEMOURS' APPLICATION PROCESS

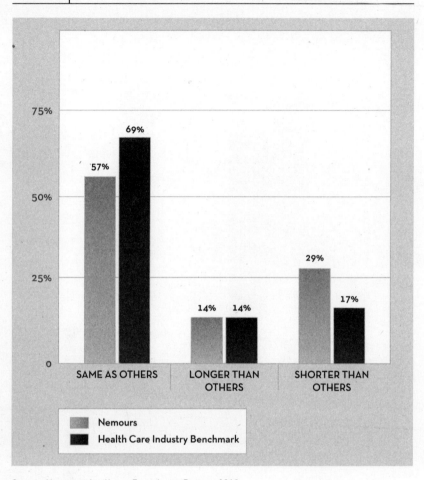

Source: Nemours Applicant Experience Report, 2012

employed full-time are a) in high demand; and b) probably don't have or don't want to take the time to apply to organizations requiring a lengthy or difficult application process. We'll learn more about this in Chapter 6 when we discuss the value of continuous recruitment.

HOW DOES NEMOURS COMMUNICATE DIFFERENTLY?

Beckler and her team explained that they rely on applicant tracking systems and other standard HR technology like most mid-sized or enterprise employers. In the case of recruiting associates for NCH, in which nearly 100,000 applied for just a few hundred positions, it would have been impossible to contact each individual applicant. Nemours relies on automation, but they use it more efficiently than the rest of the industry.

The graph in Figure 5.10 represents those applicants who are contacted by Nemours after submitting their application versus those

FIGURE 5.10 | NEMOURS' COMMUNICATION WITH CANDIDATES

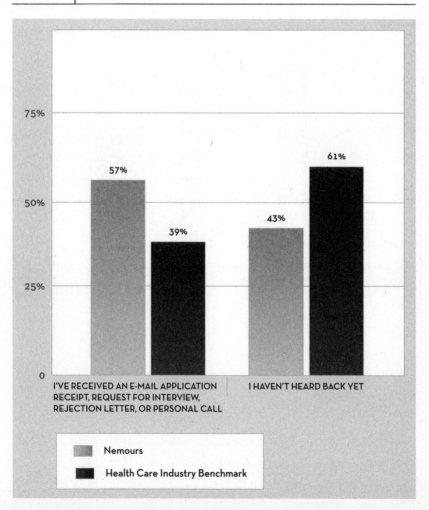

Source: Nemours Applicant Experience Report, 2012

who are not contacted within a four-week time period. There are two things unique about Nemours here. First, there are a high percentage of applicants who receive an e-mail when they are rejected. Second, Nemours candidates are notified of their status after four weeks at a much higher rate than the rest of the industry. Forty-three percent of Nemours candidates say they have not been contacted compared to 61 percent of competitors. Among that 43 percent are applicants who either did not see Nemours' initial receipt of application message or did not consider the receipt to be communication. In any case, Nemours is significantly outpacing the industry on this important measure.

Many job seekers state that one of the biggest frustrations with the application process is the fact there is rarely any one-to-one, human interaction unless you're lucky enough to be selected for a screening or an interview. Marilyn Kmetz, a senior recruiter for Nemours in the Delaware Valley sympathizes. "Nemours' culture is built on respect and we extend that respect to those who are seeking to join our team," said Kmetz. "We keep the lines of communication open to applicants throughout the process, particularly when they call to check on the status of their application." That's a simple courtesy many job seekers will tell you is welcomed but rare in the digital era of job recruitment.

*   *   *

Nemours and AIG remind us that preserving a reputation and building an employment brand is often as simple as being candid, courteous, and as responsive as possible. When companies hold themselves to those virtues and integrate them into their processes and application technologies, they'll very likely see a better candidate pool over time. But as in any marketing campaign, refining a candidate experience or employment brand must begin with a robust understanding of what motivates the consumer of the message. Measuring each step of the experience—from applicants' perceptions of your organization before they apply and their preferred job search behavior, to what attracts them to the job description and turns them off in the process itself—provides the impetus for making changes to a recruitment strategy.

CHAPTER 6

Recruiting in the Digital Era

The history of human resources can be described simply as a constant evolution. A century ago, HR wasn't even called HR, and a short time before then, such a function didn't even exist. Pre-twentieth century, business owners controlled all decisions affecting workers. However, the emergence of organized labor movements created a business need for professionals to sit at the intersection of the organizations' interests and those of human capital. By the 1950s and 1960s, labor-relations departments had uniformly transformed into organized personnel functions—masters of compliance and transactional tasks. And by the 1980s and 1990s, as globalization and information technologies changed business reality, HR became a full-fledged discipline dedicated to areas such as management strategy, organizational culture, and strategic recruitment.[1]

As in every preceding era, the twenty-first century HR department remains in transition. To a degree, modern practitioners are still shedding the widespread misperceptions that they are merely "compliance police," "payroll people," or "complaint box administrators." While these functions are critical to an organization's ability to operate on a day-to-day basis and should not be downplayed, the public's perception of HR departments seems to be more reminiscent of the 1960s definition than an accurate representation of the role they play today. Increasingly, HR is not a group of transactional workers, but a dynamic, strategic operation that can significantly affect business outcomes.

From the ATS to the electronic payroll and time cards, technology has allowed HR to automate many of its most energy- and time-consuming processes. This freeing up of resources allows the modern HR manager to become less of a "task master" and more of a "strategic consultant." As a result, the market for human capital management (HCM) technology is growing fast. Analysts at William Blair note that from August 2011 through July 2012, there were 90 transactions in HR technology mergers and acquisitions valued at $8.9 billion dollars. This tracks closely with total corporate spending on HCM. Lisa Rowan of International Data Corporation (IDC) told the *Wall Street Journal* that spending was $7.5 billion in 2011, rising to around $8 billion in 2012, and is expected to reach $11 billion by 2015.[2] Hundreds of major vendors make up the HCM space, which offers an ever-growing list of services covering the entire employee lifecycle: candidate screening and assessment, workforce planning, onboarding, performance management, payroll and benefits administration, learning and development, wellness, and online and social recruiting.

"HR technology solutions have evolved beyond simple automation of human resources business processes," wrote William Blair's Robert Metzger and Andrew Arno for their HR Technology Insights newsletter. "The combination of cloud-based consumer-friendly application interfaces with industrial-strength analytic capabilities is enabling widespread adoption across the enterprise (from rank-and-file employees to the CEO)."[3]

The analytic functions found in many of these products are often crucial to modern HR practitioners. We noted in the Introduction that, despite the fact everyone seems to like the promise of big data in human capital, the current skills composition of the HR workforce often prevents effective adoption. However, when the statisticians' work is outsourced and repackaged into simple-to-use, web-based applications and dashboards, it becomes possible for an HR manager to apply a data-driven approach without mastering the complex processes underlying effective analysis. It's important to reiterate what this type of analysis can do for a firm. For example, a 2010 study of nearly 200 large companies found that firms adopting "data-driven decision making" are more productive by a factor of 5 to 6 percent compared to those that did not.[4] An additional study found that when companies simultaneously adopted HCM, performance pay, and HR analytics practices, they tended to see a large productivity premium.[5]

The need for talent acquisition and recruitment analytics tools continues to grow within the broader HCM market. Forrester Research values the recruitment applications market at above $1 billion dollars, growing at a healthy rate of 8 percent annually.[6] In the context of skills shortages in high-growth fields and corresponding "recruitment challenges," the activity in this sector is unsurprising. CEOs know that addressing human capital needs and predicting the skills competencies necessary for growth and innovation three to five years into the future are essential in the knowledge economy. HR is most naturally in the position to be the resource for C-level leaders in this regard. This chapter suggests that when recruiting in the digital era, technology isn't just a time-saving crutch; it's an information resource that allows companies to reach skilled candidates more efficiently. In Chapter 1, we introduced several strategies for mitigating any real, perceived, or potential skills shortages. In this chapter, we return to a few strategies on that list, all of which are now actionable with the help of new technologies and data analytics: planning and managing a talent pipeline, using predictive labor supply and demand data to influence recruiting and business development, and finally, removing barriers to application for high-value candidates by adapting to the growing use of mobile technology. Recruiting in the digital age should ideally make filling ordinary, low-skill jobs more efficient and lessen the time and cost of tough-to-fill roles. And yet, many HR departments are still slow to adopt the tools that empower the process. The following results are from a nationwide survey of HR managers conducted by CareerBuilder in 2012. Each question sets the stage for the three topics we'll discuss.

CONTINUOUS RECRUITMENT

Does your organization have a talent pipeline or a pool of potential job candidates they can tap into at any time when a position opens?

▶ Yes: 52 percent

▶ No: 48 percent

Hard-to-fill positions are even harder to fill when an organization starts from scratch. An unexpected job vacancy can either leave talent management leaders scrambling or prepared to tap into their existing network of qualified, interested candidates who've opted into learning more about employment opportunities for that firm.

LABOR SUPPLY

Do you routinely use data intelligence—such as identifying markets with an oversupply and undersupply of relevant talent—to plan recruitment strategies?

▶ Yes: 33 percent

▶ No: 67 percent

Of the 67 percent of HR managers who do not use data intelligence, about one-third stated they preferred using strategies that have worked in the past. More than half, however, either said they don't know how to access that information or feel that type of information is limited.

MOBILE JOB SEARCH

Are you using mobile technology to recruit job candidates?

▶ Yes: 22 percent

▶ No: 65 percent

▶ No, but plan to in 2013: 13 percent

According to Cisco, nearly one-fifth of all consumer Internet traffic will originate from mobile devices by 2016.[7] Google data shows that 31 percent of all searches for jobs came from mobile devices in November 2012—up from just 8 percent in November 2010. But most options for applying to jobs via mobile technology are simply lagging behind this unmistakable trend. A wide majority of companies don't provide mobile-friendly careers pages, job recommendation e-mails, or apply options, further complicating their ability to reach the widest applicant pool.

CONTINUOUS RECRUITMENT AND TALENT NETWORKS

Proactive is a classically overused term in recruitment and the business world in general. How many times have you been told to not be "reactive" when an unexpected event occurs? If you were adequately prepared, the consequences—lost revenue and productivity—may have been mitigated. It's an aphorism of hindsight. We always want to do things differently after a misstep is made, but that's easier said than done.

But in the context of talent acquisition, there's still a good reason to give "proactive" a permanent place in the business lexicon. Most organizations do not allocate resources to continuous recruitment—the process of sourcing and connecting with candidates even if there are no current open positions that suit their interests or abilities. In fact, in a CareerBuilder survey of more than 2,500 hiring and HR managers, only 57 percent said their companies continuously recruit. However, it would be unfair to place blame on HR professionals themselves. Many departments suffered major cutbacks during the recession. As a result, stretched resources were typically directed toward essential, day-to-day HR functions, and networking and recruiting to accommodate future demand remains low on their list of priorities.

However, for those organizations who do continuously recruit, there are very real benefits:

▶ Seventy-two percent of employers who continuously recruit report they have reduced time-to-hire, with 41 percent stating it shaves off at least three weeks on average.

▶ Forty-one percent of employers who continuously recruit report the strategy lowers cost-per-hire. One in five says it results in saving $1,000 or more per hire. And that figure doesn't account for prevention of additional losses of revenue or productivity that often result from extended vacancies.

Suppose a highly skilled web developer at your organization relocates for a better opportunity. Past experience tells the recruiter that it can take anywhere between one to three months to find an adequate replacement. This can come at a significant cost to the company, as we've discussed in prior chapters. The developer's colleagues have to pick up the slack, even if the additional work isn't their core competency. Inefficiencies can lead to lower productivity, strained relationships with internal and external clients, burned-out workers, and ultimately, lower revenue.

But say the recruiter already has a list of thirty candidates ready to show the hiring manager the moment a position opens. For skilled roles especially, starting with a baseline of prospects is always easier than starting from scratch. The list is what we call a talent pipeline—a network of qualified, interested candidates with the skills and experience that match an organization's current and future hiring needs. People within a talent pipeline could be made up of previous interviewees who were not hired initially, individuals who met recruiters through networking or career fairs, or even candidates who submit resumes knowing there are no openings at the time but are interested in working for the employer one day. A pipeline can also include candidates who weren't right for the job for which they applied, but may be perfect for similar job listings they did not see.

As we mentioned in the chapter's introduction, only half of hiring managers state they have access to a talent pipeline. So how can recruiters begin developing a relevant network? If the only exposure recruiters have to prospects are the names they collect through job postings, they'll be severely limited. As a solution, some recruiters post job openings that aren't actually available as a method of lead generation. But this violates the trust of job seekers. People expect that the jobs they apply to are real. If done subversively, this method of sourcing won't be effective in brand building or attracting workers who are only passively interested in exploring new career opportunities. Many recruiters choose to leverage their existing applicant tracking systems by scanning the database of resumes from recent applicants. But there are limitations to this tactic, as candidates in the ATS pool may have been singularly interested in one position, or may not be actively interested in the organization itself or other job opportunities within the organization. Applicant tracking systems, generally speaking, are built for workflow, not engagement, re-engagement, or job search optimization.

The solution in this case is to think beyond standard tools for recruiting and hiring. One such web-based tool is Talent Network, a recruiting platform offered by CareerBuilder as a supplement to job boards, company career sites, and applicant tracking systems. It's a system that uses years' worth of job search behavioral data to ensure recruiters are exposed to qualified candidates on a continual basis.

At its simplest level, a company's network is a standalone website integrated with an ATS and company career page that allows prospective candidates to join with an e-mail address, upload resumes, and opt-in for updates and job recommendations when positions of interest become available. If there happens to be an open position that fits the candidate's profile, they can also apply for the job directly. Candidates find a Talent Network site via organic search or through "Join" links located on the organization's website, social media channels, or targeted ads.

We sat down with Heidi Bertelli, director of talent acquisition and strategy for Sunrise Senior Living, to discuss her continuous recruitment efforts and use of her Talent Network site. Based in Virginia, Sunrise is the second largest provider of assisted living and independent living senior housing in the U.S. With nearly 300 facilities internationally, Bertelli and her team are in constant need of skilled nursing professionals—one of the occupations most closely associated with the skills gap. To date, Bertelli has built a network of some 80,000 medical professionals interested in employment at Sunrise.

"I have candidates that are already interested before I spend a dollar on advertising," she said. "Before I do anything, I look at our talent pipeline."

In our interview, Bertelli identified three other aspects of the tool that help Sunrise reach this target audience:

- ▶ Search-engine optimized job listings allow job seekers to find vague or company-specific job titles that typically don't match commonly used keywords.

- ▶ Getting into the Sunrise network is as simple as a name, e-mail, location, and desired job title, allowing prospective candidates to land on the company's radar without making them work to do so. Resume uploads are often optional.

- ▶ Sunrise's Talent Network site is a direct channel for communicating their employment brand.

Let's explore each of these items in more detail.

BETTER JOB MATCHING

There is often a gap between the technology HR pros want job seekers to use and the technology or processes the job seekers are actually using. Knowing this, a business can do one of two things: 1) Play by their own terms and be content with the applicants that find them on job boards or company career pages; or 2) cover the technology gap and discover relevant job seekers on platforms they are most likely to use. As we said earlier, the average candidate uses 15 resources to search for jobs, and many times, the methods are quite basic. "The first thing people often do when looking for a job is log in to a search engine, type a job title and the word 'job' after it," Bertelli told us. "They're often not going to job boards; they're not going to company job sites." In fact, more than two-thirds of job seekers list search engines as a primary source for initial job market research.

This posed a problem for Bertelli and her recruiting team. Job seekers weren't likely to find Sunrise jobs through simple Google searches.

Until recently, a Sunrise Senior Living sales professional was called a "director of community relations." Imagine a job seeker using the search "sales professional jobs in Naperville, Illinois." The odds of that person finding a Sunrise position are pretty weak, despite the fact Sunrise has a facility in that particular Chicago suburb. Nowhere in the job title are the words "sales," "professional," or even something tangentially related like "marketing." To the lay person, a director of community relations may sound like a social coordinator or public relations professional. But most importantly, the search engine optimization (SEO) of the old Sunrise job titles weren't designed to accommodate how people were browsing sales jobs. Even if someone typed "sales in assisted living" into their search engine, the Sunrise job wouldn't have ranked well.

It was a blind spot, but one that they fixed. It's also a challenge far from unique to Sunrise.

To understand why interacting with job titles can be frustrating for job seekers and companies alike, we have to understand how job titles work. In a perfect world, job titles would be standardized. No matter where you work in the private sector, your title would be as easily understood as a military rank. In essence, a job title should communicate two pieces of information: function and seniority. For instance, it's not that hard to guess what a junior B2B marketing manager does. He's probably low-ranking, and most certainly has something to do with the day-to-day B2B marketing efforts. Fairly simple, right? But our working world is not that logical, as anyone who's worked for more than a few months can tell you. Ranks are subjective between firms and even between departments at the same company. A vice president at one company may equate to middle management at a larger firm. Moreover, step into some firms and you might count more associate vice presidents than managers or directors. Even the implicit meaning of management seems to have disappeared. An HR manager doesn't necessarily have subordinates to manage, even if the term "manager" historically implies "someone's boss." In the knowledge and information economy, managing processes often takes the place of managing people.

The functions of a job title can be perplexingly vague, as well. Try to figure out the more simplified job titles for the following, real-life titles as listed in job advertisements:

▶ Reminiscence care coordinator

▶ Conversation architect

▶ PT RN NS 12–6

▶ Front end ninja

These jobs are, respectively: Alzheimer's nurse; digital marketing manager; part-time registered nurse, night shift: 12 a.m. to 6 a.m.; and IT developer.

It's very likely some job seekers will discern the functions of these jobs by just looking at the title. Ninja has recently become a popular catchall for many IT specialist positions. However, when so many job seekers are using simple Google searches to locate jobs in their area, ambiguity can be a problem. The more confusing your job title, the less likely the job seeker will find you in the initial phases of their search. Using terms like "ninja" or using outdated job titles hurt postings simply because few candidates search that way. It may seem easier to just change vague job titles to something more functional. But even doing that doesn't guarantee job seekers' keywords will match the description.

Talent Network sites circumvent this SEO problem through a data-driven approach. The software takes job search behavior collected by CareerBuilder to match job descriptions with relevant terms. The average job seeker will use anywhere between 7 and 10 different search terms for a typical search query. By studying this mountain of data, analysts are able to connect all the terms and phrases nurses use to search for jobs in their industry, and then tie that back to Sunrise positions. When Bertelli posts a nursing job, the candidate, using a range of titles and terms, will in all likelihood see the Sunrise network ranked high on the results. In a large demographic market, this can make a world of difference. Not every organization needing nurses is able to link their career site to the first page of Google. With that advantage, Bertelli's goal of building a robust talent pipeline is all the more simple.

When job seekers find Sunrise's network, they're given the option to apply for jobs immediately or simply join the site, where they provide a name, e-mail, area of interest, and a resume if desired, and wait for one of Bertelli's recruiters to be in touch.

Within one year, 90 percent of all employers using Talent Network find their search terms listed on the first page of search engine results.

Efficiently Connecting to High-Skill Labor

In a low-supply, high-demand market, it makes sense that the skilled laborer should have the bargaining power. If an employer is unwilling to play by the talent's terms, they're likely to lose them to an organization also competing for that talent. This is the basic economic principle underlying why certain niche occupations in today's labor market are (or should be) witnessing rising wages. Bertelli explained to us that the same principle of preferential treatment holds true for other aspects of the hiring process.

"Does a nurse who is in high demand want to upload her resume and get back to work or does she want to complete a thirty-minute application? It's a very competitive market, right?" she said. "So we've created a culture where nurses don't feel like they have to do what the average person has to do to find a job." Bertelli noted that nurses understand they're in high demand and expect to be treated as such. "They want employers to reach out to them and say, 'Come work for me,'" she said.

Because joining a Talent Network site takes between one and three minutes, nurses are much more likely to appreciate this style of job search.

Many times, nurses looking to make a career change are already employed full-time. If their services are in as much demand as we are to believe, they shouldn't have to jump through hoops. Experienced nurses in the market can easily receive multiple job offers simultaneously. The employer that caters to their limited time and cuts straight to the issues nurses care about—organizational culture, work–life balance, compensation—will stand a much greater chance of attracting top talent in the field.

This is of course true for high-value positions in all industries. The "cut to the chase" mentality is important for this class of job seeker. More generally, the recession ignited nostalgia for how the job search used to work before the Internet and the ATS. Bertelli noted that candidates remember when getting a job required filling out an application at the physical location, completing an on-site interview on the same visit, and knowing one's odds of landing a job almost instantly. While the efficiencies and ease that modern web recruitment tools bring to the process aren't going away, alternative technologies such as Talent Network are inducing HR to make recruiting more about person-to-person interaction again.

"We're in the process of changing expectations; meaning, it's about meeting in the middle of technology and what an applicant's experience used to be," she said.

Prior to setting up their search-engine optimized Talent Network, Sunrise noticed that a lot of prospective candidates were going to the career page, browsing jobs, starting applications, and eventually quitting before finishing. High drop-off rates limit prospective talent pools, and in turn, limit the odds of a recruiter finding quality candidates for highly skilled positions. This is an applicant experience challenge that continuous recruitment helps eliminate.

ENGAGE ALREADY-INTERESTED CANDIDATES

Talent pipelines are only as useful as their day-to-day applications. A database of names and resumes (representing an organization's warm or interested candidates) is great in its own right. Recruiters can browse profiles to see where network members are currently employed, what jobs they're interested in, and the skills they possess. An open position can be filled simply by reaching out to candidates who were only a vacancy away from being a perfect hire. On a mass scale, members of a network can opt-in for automated job matching e-mails. These notifications let prospects know when there's a new opening in an area that is relevant to their interests and experiences, which greatly reduces the time-to-hire and lowers cost-per-hire. But even this underplays the potential uses of an active talent pipeline.

"Most of our recruiters are using the network as a way to keep passive job seekers warm," said Bertelli. "I see it as a huge opportunity. We have 80,000 people who are interested in our organization, which means they're willing to receive messages from us. The things we can do with that platform are endless."

Talent Network is a platform for brand messaging and candidate engagement. It's not spam or junk mail; candidates have opted in to the messaging and can stop it at anytime. If used wisely, employers can leverage the network to crystallize their image as an employer of choice. When the right position does open for an individual in the network, they are more likely to apply. And because they're already part of the network, the organization will be more likely to review their experience and invite them to interviews. This targeted communication channel allows employers to personally invite candidates to job fairs, engage with company social media pages, or share recent company news and upcoming opportunities. Additionally, member organizations can import years' worth of archived candidate information from their ATS and re-engage past candidates.

Engagement is an essential part of getting the most out of talent pipelines. Over-communicating carries risks and will lead to drop-offs, but smart, targeted messages can feed candidates' intrinsic desire to learn more about your company.

Bertelli told us that communicating an employment brand to a large audience that's willing and eager to listen is an important goal for Sunrise. As such, she recently called for an employment brand overhaul to simplify the company's message. "Our value proposition [doesn't include perks such as] shift differential pay or sign-on bonuses. What we offer is a balance a lot [of workers] in the profession want: a Monday through Friday, nine-to-five job where our nurses are really the difference in our organization. You get a chance to develop true relationships, long-term relationships with residents. Oftentimes, that's the piece that nurses say they're missing when they're working for a competitor. We build our employment brand and recruiting process around that message."

THE USES OF LABOR SUPPLY AND DEMAND DATA

Continuous recruitment can expedite the process of recruiting hard-to-fill positions, but it doesn't change the fact that filling a specific requisition can be an immensely frustrating task. There are always going to be openings that take longer than others to fill. There will always be elusive skills that require more than the basic job advertising tactics to secure. So what other avenues do talent acquisition professionals traverse when left with their shoulders shrugged?

Let's explore this question by looking at a particularly difficult position to fill: chemical engineers. This subset of engineering is the definition of a high level STEM job. Workers apply principals of physics, chemistry, basic engineering, and technology to manufacture a variety of industrial products, from gasoline to synthetic rubbers and plastics. In 2012, according to EMSI, there were about 29,000 chemical engineering jobs in the U.S., representing just 0.0002 of the nation's working population. So this is surely a small corner of the U.S. labor market. As such, these workers are well compensated, fetching about $45 per hour for their work. The field is growing at a rate of about 2 percent a year.

Yet on a national level, it would seem the supply of chemical engineers is sufficient for demand. There are more than 8,500 graduates in chemical engineering programs each year—a number that has gone up considerably post-recession. In 2008, for instance, 6,600 chemical engineering degrees were conferred annually. Many of these professionals will end up finding jobs in different engineering fields that have more abundant opportunities. In 2012, the unemployment rate for chemical engineers was 2.7 percent. This raises the question: If a recruiter for this occupation says he's facing a skills shortage because he can't find enough chemical engineers, is he looking in the right places?

In Chapter 1, we introduced the idea that skills shortages are often seen and felt most at the local level. For certain jobs, companies really do have a shortage of qualified workers in their home market. This is a perennial structural challenge, one that existed long before the recession. The obvious solution is to look beyond one's own backyard. Don't have a training budget but need that tech professional who knows Hadoop? Or a veteran surgical technician? Then you should start scouring nearby locales. Seems like a no brainer. But when advertising and recruitment budgets are on the line, justifying where to look requires more than a map or a "good hunch."

Fortunately, the era of big data has given a facelift to a classic solution: Study the labor market—the supply of labor, the regional hubs of demand, the appropriate levels of compensation. Armed with this information, a recruiter can not only decide where to spend, but also inform management as to whether or not the salary package will attract the needed talent. It can guide a company toward offering relocation packages to entice out-of-market candidates. Until the past few years, this information was tough for the average recruiter to access. And if you remember the stat introduced at the outset of the chapter, a lot of HR pros still don't know where to get this information or entirely fail to see its usefulness. The BLS has a wealth of information on occupations and industry employment, but analyzing that data, which isn't always the most recently available or easy to breakdown by region, is a cumbersome chore most HR pros don't want to—or aren't trained to-tackle. However, this type of analysis is the antidote to flying blind in a tight labor market. Armed with supply and demand statistics about specific skills, job titles, and labor pools, a recruiter can set reasonable expectations for the process and literally change the way they look at the map.

The Supply & Demand Portal, a CareerBuilder data tool introduced in 2011, makes the acquisition and comprehension of this data relatively easy. The portal provides a snapshot of a region's labor landscape. Users simply enter a skill, job title, or occupation along with their region, and the software draws a comprehensive dashboard and series of exportable reports illustrating supply, demand, and labor pressure for their query. The data covers 95 percent of all online postings and estimates the available labor pool by combining BLS and other government data with college completion rates. The labor supply data is aggregated by EMSI. To see how the data can be used, let's return to the chemical engineer example.

Say you're trying to fill a senior process engineer position for a small manufacturer in the Minneapolis–St. Paul region. The metropolitan area has a population of more than three million people, but according to EMSI, less than 300 employed chemical engineers. There's only one nearby college chemical engineering program, which produces about 125 graduates a year. What are the odds of grabbing

FIGURE 6.1 | RESULTS FROM CAREERBUILDER'S SUPPLY & DEMAND PORTAL FOR CHEMICAL ENGINEERS IN THE TWIN CITIES AREA

one of these currently employed or freshly minted engineers? The portal is designed to help answer that question. Figure 6.1 shows the first thing you see when you search for chemical engineers in the Twin Cities.

The data shown in this search covers two years, but can be narrowed to cover short-term trends. It shows that 286 chemical engineering jobs were posted in total over this time frame. The supply number indicates the number of candidates active in CareerBuilder's resume database in that time frame, allowing you to instantly look at their job history and skills information. The total available workforce figure estimates the number of people in the region that could potentially fill your position. But this figure mostly includes already employed workers, thus shrinking the size of the pool that may even consider interviewing with you. Finally, the hiring indicator is a labor pressure indicator derived from an algorithm that weighs multiple supply and demand factors for the occupation. The lower the number on the scale, the more difficult the recruiting task will typically be. In this case, a hiring measure of 24 indicates that 76 percent of all other occupations in the Twin Cities are easier to recruit than chemical engineers.

Your sense that this was going to be a tough requisition to close is confirmed. However, that's all just a snapshot. The portal allows users to go a few layers deeper. In the Demand tab for instance, you can see exactly how many other openings similar to yours are available in the area broken down by the month, and identifies companies seeking similar talent. For example, you'll find that the large regional employer 3M posts the most jobs for chemical engineers in the Twin Cities area. Moreover, the tab shows demand for chemical engineers nationwide over the specified timeframe, illustrating that between June 2012 and May 2013, Minnesota demanded about as many chemical engineers as New York State.

At this juncture, given the tight labor pressure, it is wise to broaden the parameters of your search. Looking at the whole of the U.S. market for chemical engineers, the portal calculates the easiest cities to recruit from based on the supply of active job seekers (see Figure 6.2).

Note that this often differs from the regions with the largest total workforce. With its robust energy industry and major companies like Honeywell, CH2M Hill, and Chevron, Texas employs 17 percent of the nation's chemical engineers. However, labor pressure data suggests you'll have a better chance getting someone to move to Minnesota from Riverside, California, or Ann Arbor, Michigan. Since the latter mirrors Minnesota's harsh winters a bit more than Florida or California's sunny days, perhaps efforts should be redirected toward the rust belt.

SETTING EXPECTATIONS AND ENGAGING IN REAL WORKFORCE ANALYTICS

The portal isn't a mess of raw data; it has tools for sorting and analysis. If a recruiter or hiring manager knows what her needs are, she doesn't need to be an analyst or statistician to find meaning in her search. We talked to Tom Newmaster, president of Corporate Staffing Services about the uses of labor data available on the Supply & Demand Portal. His firm relies on providing both job seeker clients and employers with relevant information as quickly as possible. "We use all the surveys from the BLS and similar information, but this is just more accurate

Top Job Posters

Company	
Honeywell International Inc.	413
Ch2m Hill Companies, Ltd.	280
E.I. Dupont India Private Limited	206
Koch Industries, Inc.	167
Merck & Co., Inc.	143
Chevron Corporation	125
Ashland Inc.	125
3M Company	112
The Dow Chemical Company	109
Koch Companies, Inc.	104

Easiest Metro Areas to Recruit

- Riverside, California Area
- Tampa/St. Petersburg, Florida Area
- Miami/Fort Lauderdale Area
- Sacramento, California Area
- Ann Arbor, Michigan Area
- Greensboro-High Point, North Carolina Area
- Greater Los Angeles Area
- Cincinnati Area
- Phoenix, Arizona Area
- Washington D.C. Metro Area

and direct," he said. "With our business, urgency is key, and the faster I get results the faster I can convey that information to the employer and the candidate. Timing is everything."

Labor data is popular among staffing and recruiting professionals, because it allows them to track geographic locations of top talent and use that information to create buy-in with potential candidates and employers. Newmaster says labor pressure data is his way of setting expectations for his clients. If the offer sheet is too low, he's up front in telling the employer where the salary needs to be. If a hiring manager pushes back and says they can't offer it, Newmaster runs a compensation report showing what other employers in the region are paying for similar skills and experience. Inversely, the compensation data can be used to convince a reticent candidate into taking an offer once shown his salary comes in above market rate. If the employer is after a niche skill set, Newmaster uses a report on regional supply to estimate the time it would take to find a candidate locally, which often leads to a green light to bring talent in from out of market.

Gordon Frutiger of AIG contends that labor supply data boosts the credibility of his recruiters within the organization, noting that before the big data capabilities of Supply & Demand, they had to rely primarily on anecdotal experience when communicating with hiring managers. "It takes information out of the anecdotal and makes it tangible, objective data," he said. "With hiring managers there is a trust factor and respect factor built in [the data] so that they look at you as a talent adviser. They often have never seen information like this before and leave meetings with a better appreciation for marketplace realities."

However, Frutiger said the real value in tools like Supply & Demand or EMSI's Analyst tool, which provides labor supply forecasting data, is that they bring talent acquisition closer to actual workforce planning. "In my mind, most everyone talks about workforce planning in the wrong way—it's all really just rearranging the chairs on the deck. It's managing job requisitions throughout the year, but that's not workforce planning," he said. "Real planning is taking data X number of years behind and taking forecasting data Y number of years forward and mapping out where, geographically, you'll be able to fill certain jobs and job categories."

Frutiger sees this type of information as critical to questions of employee relocation or migrating entire departments, such as IT support, to areas of the country more amenable to regional skill sets. In other words, it allows traditional HR to step closer to being seen as true internal consultants.

THE JOB MARKET IN THE PALM OF YOUR HANDS

The year 2010 marked a significant technological milestone. In the fourth quarter, according to the International Data Corporation, smartphone shipments surpassed that of PCs.[8]

The moment reinforced what we all knew to be true: The mass popularity and increased affordability of mobile devices will forever change the way the world communicates and consumes information. As a result of this pervasive, Teutonic shift, the mobile takeover is causing the most significant change to the World Wide Web since its inception. The change is fast and incontrovertible. Most importantly, as of early 2013, the shift had only just begun:

▸ As a result of the proliferation of mobile phones and tablets, Cisco projects there will be 18.9 billion network connections globally by 2016—up from 10.3 billion in 2011. That's an average of about 2.5 Internet connections per person on earth.[9]

▸ By 2016, mobile phones and tablets will account for nearly one-fifth of all Internet traffic, spread across nearly 4.5 billion mobile users globally. A 2013 survey of U.S.-based companies found that 23 percent of the participants' web hits derived from mobile devices—a 283 percent increase from just two years earlier.[10]

▶ Mobile users are always connected and often integrate smartphone Internet use with other activities. Nielsen Media found that a majority of Americans regularly browse the web on their smartphones or tablets while watching television.[11]

This is not a trend. It is the new reality. "Mobile devices will claim more and more media time per day, while TV, print, and radio will slowly lose ground to digital media," said Noah Elkin, principal analyst for eMarketer. "For marketers, half the battle of staying relevant is showing up in the right place and on the right platform."[12]

As we all know by now, job recruitment is marketing. Elkin's advice is just as applicable to your HR department as it is to executives on Madison Avenue. The ever-increasing share of Internet traffic coming from mobile technology is radically changing the job search process.

▶ As mentioned earlier in this chapter, searches for "jobs" on Google have increased exponentially. In November 2012, Google reported that 31 percent of searches for "jobs" originated from mobile devices—up from 17 percent in 2011 and 8 percent in 2010.

▶ On job sites like CareerBuilder.com, one third of all traffic comes from mobile devices and tablets as of early 2013—up from just a few percent two years prior.

As we indicated at the beginning of the chapter, however, the mobile revolution has left many HR departments flat footed. Countless companies have mobile recruiting "dead zones"—a digital barrier to job seekers' ability to learn more about a company and its career opportunities, as well as their ability to apply for a position from their mobile device. An experienced talent acquisition professional would never purposely choose to cut out 20 to 30 percent of the available talent pool, but that's exactly what millions of companies are doing by ignoring the mobile job search experience.

So what's the hold up? Why is the HR world slow to react to the new reality of the job search?

We hear time and time again from HR managers, "We don't want to invest in a mobile-friendly career site, because not enough of our applicants want to search or apply that way."

There are a few problems with this line of reasoning. First, it very well may contradict their companies' own mobile statistics. If you're a recruiter or HR manager, equip yourself with the most relevant data. A simple Google analytics account will illustrate current and potential demand for mobile job search. Find out the percentage of visits to your career page originating from mobile devices, or go a step further and look at top landing pages for your site coming from mobile traffic. Then check the bounce rate—the number of visitors who immediately abandon the site upon loading.

Even if mobile visitors are scant, it's still not sufficient reason to sit on your hands. Mobile recruitment is very much an instance of "If you build it, they will come." Job seekers can't make mobile technology an important part of the process if most companies prevent them from efficiently browsing careers or applying using their mobile devices. Of companies who have mobile-optimized career sites, one in five said more than 20 percent of their applications are already originating from mobile devices. One in ten said more than half of their applications derive from mobile users. Moreover, job seeker demand for mobile job search is very high. One recent survey suggested that 86 percent of job seekers said they'd apply for a job on a mobile device if the option was available. When CareerBuilder.com enhanced its mobile apply option in 2012, allowing job seekers to apply with a simple lead form or resume upload, applications from mobile devices increased by 50 percent.

Let's say you have a well-designed, touch-optimized career site that can be used comfortably on a smartphone or tablet. You are already better than most businesses. However, there is one more barrier: the application itself. After finding a job for which the candidate wants to apply, she'll often encounter an alarmingly long application process. As noted in Chapter 5, 15-page applications are not recommended on desktops. But they're an absolute deal breaker on mobile devices. People's thumbs and attention spans aren't agile enough to tolerate them. Our research suggests that 40 percent of mobile candidates immediately drop-off the website after encountering a non-mobile-friendly application process, and the other 60 percent aren't likely to complete a clunky ATS-based application even if they start. Sun Communities, an operator of RV resorts and manufactured home communities, noticed a similar trend for their job listings. Marc Farrugia, a human resources manager for Sun, told *USA Today* that the candidates "who are a little more cutting edge" are exactly the candidates he wants, and are the most likely to be using mobile technology.[13]

Finally, the media used to link candidates to the application often poses an unforeseen hurdle. Many job seekers sign up for e-mail job recommendations through company career sites. Because more than 40 percent of e-mail is now opened on mobile devices, HR must double-check that those e-mails are mobile friendly, as well.

Smartphones and tablet devices marry convenience and immediacy. Because users have unlimited accessibility to the web whenever they want, wherever they want, mobile technologies are essentially rewiring job seeker behavior. Consumers demand transactions that can begin and end with a few clicks. You can't count on all candidates, especially high-skilled, already employed workers, to revisit your career site on a desktop platform. While many services will invite the job seeker to have the job application e-mailed so they can complete it later, offering a mobile application option—with one-click resume uploads and user-friendly screening questions—will be a standard feature in the near future. Trends overwhelmingly indicate it will be a general consumer expectation. For this reason, of all the technological developments to affect human capital management and talent acquisition in recent years, mobile recruitment is perhaps the one area companies can least afford to ignore.

CHAPTER 7

Retaining Talent in Critical Functions

In late 2012, the *Wall Street Journal's* Joseph Walker gave the world a peek at the potential uses of big data in human resources:

"For more and more companies, the hiring boss is an algorithm. The factors they consider are different than what applicants have come to expect. Jobs that were once filled on the basis of work history and interviews are left to personality tests and data analysis, as employers aim for more than just a hunch that a person will do the job well."[1]

But it's not just who "will do the job well"; it's who will stay on the job. Xerox Corp., for instance, claims to have reduced the turnover rate by one-fifth for its nearly 50,000 call center jobs after it decided to allow a big data software screening application to help make its hiring decisions. It costs $5,000 to train one employee at Xerox, so reducing attrition rates is naturally a perennial effort. Evolv, a San Francisco startup, is the company advising Xerox's new hiring system. Previously, according to Walker, Xerox based its decisions on standard factors like work history, education, and experience, but was shown that such things matter far less than the psychological profiles of candidates. Now candidates for these jobs take a 30-minute psych evaluation. As it turns out, the call-center workers most likely to stick with the job long enough for the company to see returns, according to Evolv, are people that tend to be more creative than inquisitive or empathetic.

The article generated a lot of response. In one sense, the positive results are hard to argue and provide a model for smart talent acquisition. The hiring decision relies more on the personality of the worker, based on a well-tested formula, and less on resume information and job history—items we know can be an inaccurate portrayal of the individual's potential and ability. The other side of the argument is marked by a queasy feeling. Are computers destined to take over a major portion of the talent acquisition function? And when we replace the human element, will the screening mechanisms open the door to a host of unintended discrimination issues? For instance, research has found a connection between voluntary turnover and distance from work to place of residence. But if a large demographic pool of the potential labor can't afford to live within a potential hiring radius, such benchmarks are subject to equal employment opportunity litigation. Moreover, if a lot of service jobs require applicants to pass a personality test, is it possible that large groups of people will be systematically unemployable due to a psychological makeup they largely can't control?

While measures must be taken to ensure everyone receives a fair chance, the use of technology and big data does not have to be quite so ominous. First, personality screening tests have long been a part of recruitment. The growing sophistication of data analytics tools is really all that's changing. The developments may actually be an improvement over a single hiring manager spending 30 seconds per resume in a pile of 300 resumes, or an ATS screening for certain keywords. The big data HR vendors will undoubtedly argue that their services are more accurate and fair because they eliminate subjective factors that aren't good predictors of one's ability to succeed. Moreover, data-driven screening tools are best used when they enhance the hiring manager's decision-making process, rather than replace it altogether. In other words, these tools can be honed to provide a small pool of people to interview, allowing more time for quality personal interaction.

The movement toward these types of empirical solutions is in part a response to a perpetual concern of human resource departments: "Will we be able to reduce the costs of turnover and retain our most valuable employees?" Xerox found a way that works. Undoubtedly, it will result in major cost savings, and if our research on customer service workers and tenure from Chapter 3 is to be believed, it could significantly improve their market performance in the long term. But would the hiring formula also work for jobs that are less routine and more dynamic? Would it work for high-value tech and business development professionals, whose retention may be critical to a company's growth?

Developing efficacious retention strategies is an art desperately trying to become science. Retention is a challenge that perplexes business leaders. A survey of more than 400 global C-suite and senior executives found that only 27 percent say their company excels at retaining key talent.[2]

There are countless theories on what it takes to retain workers. The truth is, there is no one-size-fits-all approach. A mix of extrinsic and intrinsic rewards, depending on the job level and function of the employee, are likely to be useful in any strategy. But overall, it is primarily a challenge of employee engagement and organizational culture building. Retention is about understanding what motivates a company's most valuable employees and being flexible enough to meet their needs. Not surprisingly, needs in this instance extend well beyond desired salary.

Research on retention is currently more in the sociopsychological space than the data-analytic space. However, in this chapter we'll use survey data, as well as discuss data-backed strategies that will help organizations retain their top employees. For instance, many companies use annual employee opinion surveys as signposts for what they can do to eliminate costly turnover. However, survey data is often misleading, and while sometimes intriguing at a cursory level, it is not always paired more rigorously with other HR data to learn more about which types of workers—salaried/hourly, long-tenured/short-tenured—are likely to stay or leave and why. We'll take a look at what one large hospitality company was able to learn after they took open-ended employee survey responses and turned them into an analytic portrait of why different employees decide to stay in their jobs.

Before we jump in, it's important to remember the lesson of Chapter 3: Before locking your organization into targeted retention strategies, make sure the returns of longer tenure are beneficial to revenue and productivity goals.

In this chapter we explore the latest research on retention strategy, including:

▸ Why retention remains a perennial top concern for employers

▸ Reasons why employees say they leave, and whether or not such data is accurate

▸ The less-explored question of why employees choose to stay with an employer

▸ Engagement strategies more likely to connect with workers and promote retention

RETENTION: HR'S NUMBER ONE CHALLENGE

We spent a lot of time in this book discussing how to find the best talent, make the recruitment process more efficient, and mend current and future skills, education, and training gaps. But none of that matters to a company if they can't maximize their returns on workers after they walk through the door. The 2012 KPMG Report "Rethinking Human Resources in a Changing World" asked 418 global executives what HR's primary focus will be over the coming three years. The overwhelming winner—by 14 percentage points—was "retaining crucial skills and experience within the business."[3] This mirrors CareerBuilder's list of top staffing challenges for 2013, in which retention ranked first among 3,000 hiring and HR managers. Not coincidentally, other challenges on the list (compensation, advancement opportunities, preventing worker burnout) are all indirectly connected to retention concerns, as they're frequently listed as causes of turnover.

Unlike "adopting data analytics," which ranked third on KPMG's list, talent retention is firmly within the wheelhouse of most HR departments. Earlier, we talked about retention in the context of measuring employee tenure. But the conversation in this chapter takes the discussion a step further. Using workforce analytics to identify which functions or individuals need longer tenures to maximize returns is a different process than actually convincing superstar talent to stay on board.

While tenure rates have increased across the board over the past decade (even in high-demand fields like IT and engineering), HR is under considerable pressure to retain their organizations' very best talent. In an era of social media connectivity, in which skills, experience, references, and connections are often made public to all prospective employers, the potential for a talent exodus can keep management up at night.

Talent retention is an important HR concern regardless of business cycle, but as with any labor market force, the recession may have exacerbated these concerns. For one, we have an environment where many employers are reticent to train and develop talent. On top of that, recruiters want the worker who fits the job description to the T—the polished diamond, so to speak. Many businesses admit they're used to doing more with less post-recession, and are often willing to wait rather than risk the bad hire. So when a high-value employee leaves, the instinct is to find that person again. As we know, recruiting skilled talent can take a while depending on the market and the recruiting strategies used. Put all these factors together and the logical question is: Why not place an emphasis on making sure more of our valued workers never want to leave?

Even if we have ample survey evidence suggesting retention concerns are paramount, it's still important to evaluate whether or not they are overstated given the labor market climate. Every month the BLS collects information on the number of jobs available, but they also measure how many people are hired and leave jobs. For instance, the total separations rate captures the number of people who leave a job in a month, regardless of the reason, represented as a percentage of the total population. The better economic signal however, is the quits rate, a measure of voluntary turnover that counts anyone who leaves for reasons other than a layoff, retirement, death, or internal transfer. The quits rate is often used as a barometer of the workforces' confidence. When more people quit their jobs, it usually means they are leaving for a different career opportunity. In the four years leading up to the recession (2004 to 2007), BLS data shows an average of 8.2 million voluntary job separations per quarter. During the following four years (2008–2011), that number plummeted to about 5.7 million per quarter. For millions of workers, thoughts of job mobility were replaced by concerns of job security. As a result, corresponding tenure rates rose during the recession and recovery.[4]

The focus on retention isn't unwarranted, however. Voluntary turnover has been inching upward since bottoming out in September 2009. The quits rate has risen from an average of 1.3 percent of total employment in 2009 to 1.6 percent of total employment in 2012 (see Figure 7.1).

While the quits rate is still below pre-recession levels, workers are growing more confident in their ability to find a new job. This is a good signal for the economy as a whole, but from the perspective of an HR manager charged with holding onto to her all-star web developers, engineers, or business intelligence analysts, it's a sign retention efforts will need a second look.

A CareerBuilder and Harris Interactive survey from early 2013 shows that while only 28 percent of private sector employers felt the

FIGURE 7.1 | VOLUNTARY QUITS RATE FROM 2006 TO 2012

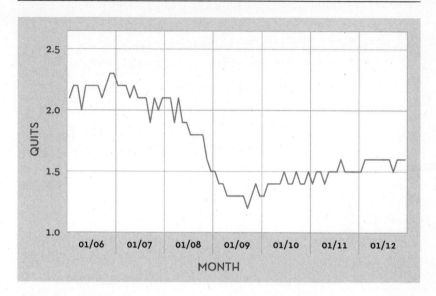

Source: BLS: JOLTS, 2012

increase in voluntary turnover at their organizations, the retention anxiety is particularly relevant for managers in three industries or sectors—IT, finance, and large health care organizations, as can be seen in Table 7.1.

The differences between these areas and the entire private sector point to where the labor market is often tightest. Employers pay a premium for highly skilled, highly trained professionals and want to keep them. On the other hand, workers in finance, IT, and health care sense their ease of career mobility is higher than low-skill laborers, and in many cases, are eager to take an opportunity elsewhere.

But not every expert thinks recruiting skilled workers from other companies is a good strategy—especially when potential internal replacements could be waiting in the wings. Our research, presented in Chapter 3, suggests that the labor flow of tech professionals can help industry laggards catch up to leaders, but there's always the risk that a

TABLE 7.1 | VOLUNTARY TURNOVER BY SECTOR

Did you see an increase in voluntary turnover at your organization in 2012?			
	Private Sector Total	Finance	IT	Health Care (Org. 500+)
Yes	28%	44%	37%	37%
No	72%	56%	63%	63%

Did top performers leave your organization in 2012?			
	Private Sector Total	Finance	IT	Health Care (Org. 500+)
Yes	32%	46%	43%	41%
No	68%	55%	57%	59%

Are you concerned about top workers leaving your organization in 2013?			
	Private Sector Total	Finance	IT	Health Care (Org. 500+)
Yes	39%	41%	53%	44%
No	62%	59%	47%	56%

Source: CareerBuilder/Harris Interactive Employer Survey, 2013

top performer at one company may not be such a superstar at the new organization. Variables such as culture, organizational structure, and people can all throw off performance. This idea was represented in the enlightening book *Chasing Stars* by Harvard professor Boris Groysberg, published in 2010. The thesis of his research took the wind out of a long-held view that said luring away star talent from competing firms is an ideal human capital strategy:

"... Exceptional performance is far less portable than widely believed. Mobile stars experienced an immediate degradation in performance. Even after five years at a new firm, star analysts who changed employers underperformed comparable star analysts who stayed put."[5]

In a knowledge economy, much emphasis is placed on the portability of the worker's skills, but it turns out, a lot of what makes exceptional workers exceptional is firm-dependent. The book started a nurture versus nature debate in the talent management world, but one inescapable idea drawn from it is that you can't always count on replacing key talent once they leave and expect similar results. The "free agent" economy—in which skilled workers move their services from company to company—is not necessarily effective for either firms or their workers. Certainly this isn't true in all cases, but it does provide a boon for advocates of stronger retention policies.

Three years later, Groysberg still sees this fallacious logic in human capital strategy, likening it to how we treat sports teams who make a big trade or sign a star free agent, only to see the investment fall flat. "Baseball fans who are paying hundreds of dollars for a ticket don't want to hear about bridge periods, and neither do board members," he said. "We've lost a lot of patience with developmental strategies in recent years. It seems like more and more in our economy, we believe that if you were a star somewhere else, we can bring you over and right away you will be a star working for us."[6]

Before we address effective retention strategies, let's review the state of retention: why workers leave, in the minds of employers; why employees say they leave; why they actually leave; how employers are responding; and why employees stay.

WHY DO EMPLOYEES LEAVE?

There's a wealth of literature and research about why workers quit. HR collects this information in the form of exit interviews. Likewise, surveys of workers tend to focus on the reasons for leaving. While limited, this information is a good starting point for developing a retention framework. In 2013, we surveyed a representative sample of more than 3,000 hiring managers and human resource managers to find out the top reasons they think talent leaves. The following sections break down the top five from that list.

Interestingly, the overwhelming number one answer, higher pay, is perhaps the least instructive on the list. We'll explore why this is so, and examine the other reasons.

HIGHER PAY

Salary/wages was the top answer in our survey, and if you just take a cursory glance at similar research, it is at the top of most lists. A late 1990s Harvard Management Update survey, for instance, found that 89 percent of managers say employees leave primarily for pay.[7] And this makes sense, right? If you work hard at a job for a certain amount of time, earn valuable experience, and happen to acquire skills along the way, you'll eventually want to be compensated for all you bring to the role. No one doubts that. The laws of supply and demand for talent compensation, which we've referenced throughout this book, apply to existing employees just as much as prospective ones. Thus, if your organization knows it is underpaying key players relative to competition for that talent, it's reasonable for them to request a raise or seek one externally.

Employees say pay matters, as well. A 2013 survey of full-time workers found increased pay and better benefits to be the top two things employers could do to entice workers to stay.

However, we're not convinced compensation is the end all and be all of retention strategies—for reasons rooted in both pragmatism and psychology.

First, let's discuss the pragmatic. Employers often use extrinsic motivators to induce retention—like salary, benefits, and perks. While those surely can be effective, especially for critical, low-in-supply skills like engineering or IT, there's only so far most companies can go before financial incentives become impractical. Ten to fifteen percent annual pay raises may in fact be the ticket for employee retention, but as a matter of pure arithmetic, most businesses will immediately dismiss this tactic, or at the very least, reserve significant bonus packages only for a small handful of valuable, high-level employees.

Fortunately, the most convincing research suggests effective retention strategy is often more about psychology than economics. Workers have a baseline expectation of what's possible. Most hard workers feel they deserve better pay, but that doesn't mean everyone in this group expects it. They may look around at other job opportunities and see similar salary ranges in the market. If they can fetch a significantly better opportunity, they'll go for it. In most cases, however, their employment decisions will first consider other questions: Do I like what I do? Am I recognized for my work by colleagues and managers? Do I see a future at this organization? Does the job provide a good quality of life?

So why do so many employers think it all has to do with pay? According to Leigh Branham, author of *The 7 Hidden Reasons Employees Leave*, it's because that's what workers tell them. He explains: "Most simply say it is about pay in the exit interview because 1) it's an answer that doesn't burn a bridge and 2) it happens to be true that most exiting employees get pay increases when they accept a job elsewhere."[8] But such exit interview explanations are not necessarily indications of why the departing worker was looking in the first place. As Branham suggests, most workers know the importance of leaving on good terms for need of references and career networks later down the line. The exiting employee may cite a great career opportunity elsewhere without ever fully addressing a negative relationship with their boss or problems with the organization itself.

Moreover, most workers are not receiving offers from other companies out of the blue. Something typically triggers the "I need a new job" thought process, which soon leads to the search, even if it is passive or infrequent. In most cases, we feel, degradation of overall job satisfaction is behind voluntary turnover. The prospect for a bigger paycheck, as persuasive as it can be, is not what causes workers to leave, even if it's often a welcome effect of the exodus.

Engaged workers who believe in their company's mission and who enjoy their work and the people they work with are much less likely to prematurely bolt from their position. It is this idea we turn to for the rest of the chapter.

POOR RELATIONSHIP WITH BOSS

Is it possible to stay in a job, let alone enjoy it, without also maintaining a good working relationship with the people you report to?

In CareerBuilder's Q1 2013 worker survey, we asked more than 3,500 full-time workers whether they planned to leave their job in 2013 or 2014. One-quarter said yes. But looking only at workers who said they had a poor or very poor opinion of their direct supervisor's performance, the percentage more than doubled to 56 percent. Conversely, 85 percent of workers who have a great opinion of their boss's performance planned to stay with their current job through at least 2014.

The relationship between job satisfaction and opinions of managerial competence is also quite strong. In fact, workers who find their boss's job performance very poor are more than five times as likely to be very dissatisfied with their job as the average worker.

While we can't show that this is directly the cause of their discontent, the difference is very significant and therefore worth noting. We're not suggesting policies exist that will magically get every employee and manager to work together harmoniously. Managerial friction is inevitable at any organization. However, HR leadership cannot disregard that job satisfaction, and in turn, retention, are largely affected by the day-to-day aspects of work. Negative consequences can be mitigated by methods like instituting clear reporting structures, frequent and transparent feedback channels that address tensions between employees and managers, and recognition programs that allow employees to feel valued for high performance regardless of their one-to-one relationship with a direct manager.

LACK OF ADVANCEMENT OPPORTUNITIES

The prospect of promotion and career progress is often used as a key motivational device in recruitment literature. It is an extrinsic reward that says to candidates, "Your future is here." There's one catch to using this as a recruitment device: You have to back it up. If the promise of an internal career path turns out to be a fantasy, or only reserved for a tiny percentage of employees, the new hires may resent the organization for having promoted it.

Most workers want to see some sort of career progress, whether that's a steady increase in salary or a new job title every X number of years. In Chapter 3, we discussed how this is particularly prevalent among young professionals, whose career roots aren't yet settled. Voluntary separations are more likely to occur when the worker senses he or she has nothing left to offer the company and the company has nothing left to offer the them.

Workers who stated that they planned to change jobs in 2013 or 2014 were asked: Are you satisfied with career advancement opportunities at your company? Their answers were as follows:

▶ Very satisfied: 3 percent

▶ Satisfied: 14 percent

▶ Neutral: 27 percent

▶ Dissatisfied: 32 percent

▶ Very dissatisfied: 23 percent

While it's inevitable that a lot of turnover will be a result of individuals pursuing new opportunities, companies need not be defeated.

There are ways to build a culture of advancement without doling out promotions to every worker the organization wants to retain. This starts with the realization that workers value a lot more than their rank. In fact, only 6 percent of full-time U.S. workers say their job title is very important to their definition of success. More than half (55 percent) say it is not at all important.

We can't confuse a better job title with job satisfaction. In this survey, more than half of all workers (58 percent) said a flexible schedule was more important than job title. Exactly half said "being able to make a difference in my job" was more important; and one-third (34 percent) said just having work that challenged them is more important. In light of these results, companies should respond by helping workers advance in other ways when there's no room for promotion, such as lateral moves, new assignments, skills training, or educational opportunities.

OVERWORKED/WORK–LIFE BALANCE

The recession left many Americans without a job, but what's often unexplored is the effects of workers who kept their position within departments that were severely downsized. Most layoffs were initially a direct response to a reduction in demand for services. Excess labor was no longer needed. To rein in costs, maintain profits, or cover operating expenses, it was not uncommon to see 15-person departments cut down to two or three workers. As the economy rebounded, many of these jobs came back.

However, not all companies are planning to return to full headcount. In fact, more than a third of all companies are still below prerecession employment levels, and 87 percent of that group will not be returning to full headcount in 2013. For many, demand doesn't warrant hiring again. However, a nearly equal amount say they are fine doing more with less.

We asked 860 employers who indicated that they were not planning on returning to full headcount in 2013 to choose all items that applied to their situation from the following list:

▸ Business is too slow; waiting for it to pick up: 51 percent

▸ We became accustomed to handling the work with less headcount: 47 percent

▸ Our business focus changed: 12 percent

▸ Company began hiring more in departments it's placing more emphasis on post-recession: 9 percent

▸ Other: 9 percent

It's possible that certain organizations were overemployed, and the recession allowed them to return to equilibrium or increase efficiency by adopting automated technologies that reduced the need for many of the positions that existed five years ago. But if this isn't the case, operating with a smaller staff can be detrimental to productivity, customer service, growth potential, and yes, retention. Thirty-eight percent of managers said they feel their current staff is burned out. That matches well with data on the workers' side of the equation. Fifty-nine percent of workers are currently stressed in their jobs and half said their workloads increased over the last 12 months.

Companies can only stretch their workforces so far before expanding payroll to accommodate increased demand. According to the survey, 46 percent of full-time workers who claim they are highly stressed say they plan to leave their job in 2013 or 2014, compared to 25 percent of workers experiencing moderate stress and 18 percent of workers experiencing no stress. While we can't attribute the source of this stress to overwork from this data alone, employers interested in retaining valued talent need to be aware of stress's potential effects and provide positive outlets.

UNHAPPY WITH ORGANIZATIONAL CULTURE

Prior scholarly research shows that an organization's values and culture—both stated and unstated—can have a strong effect on employees' eagerness to stay on board. It may not be something they always reference in an exit interview, but the business environment can severely sway overall job satisfaction. The relationship between culture and retention was illustrated empirically by researcher John Sheridan, who over a six-year period in the in the late 1980s and early 1990s followed 900 college graduates who entered six competing accounting firms in the same city.[9] After controlling for external factors that could also affect retention—like their college GPA, marital status/family obligations, compensation, and relocation—Sheridan measured correlations between a standardized list of organizational values and the median tenure of the new hires. The values were attributed to each organization based on evaluations from senior-tenured employees.

After 12 months, individuals voluntarily quit their jobs at a much faster rate (31 months) in the culture emphasizing work-task values than in the culture emphasizing interpersonal relationship values (45 months).

There's a potential downside to a culture stressing interpersonal values over work-task values: both strong and weak performers are retained. "In this culture, there was only a one month difference in their median survival times," Sheridan wrote. But in organizations that stressed work-task values, weak performers left 13 months earlier on average than strong performers. The company would have to evaluate whether the gains from retaining all new accounting employees outweighed the gains of retaining high performers for a longer period of time.

WHY DO WORKERS STAY IN A JOB?

Certainly knowing the rationale for turnover is useful. You can't plug a leak without finding the crack. But perhaps focusing on the negative—

the stated reasons for voluntary quits—isn't as instructive as finding out why people choose to stay in their jobs to begin with. The goal here, we would hope, is to develop a successful retention policy rather than a turnover prevention policy. In a past study, researchers Steel, Griffeth, and Hom, noted "the reasons people stay are not always the same reasons people leave."[10]

In the CareerBuilder survey referenced in the previous section, we asked workers what employers could do to increase retention. The majority of workers (70 percent) reported that increasing salaries is the best way to boost employee retention, while 58 percent pointed to better benefits. Other actions workers said employers should take to reduce voluntary turnover include:

▶ Provide flexible schedules: 51 percent

▶ Increase employee recognition (awards, cash prizes, company trips): 50 percent

▶ Ask employees what they want and put feedback into action: 48 percent

▶ Increase training and learning opportunities: 35 percent

▶ Provide special perks (free lunch, game room, concierge service, etc.): 26 percent

▶ Hire additional workers to ease workloads: 22 percent

▶ Provide academic reimbursement: 22 percent

▶ Carve out specific career paths and promote more: 21 percent

▶ Institute a more casual dress code: 14 percent

Knowing what workers want most is important, but there is a key limitation to this question. To workers, most of whom plan on staying in their job for the next two years, such a question can be viewed primarily as a "wish list." Receiving any one of these items very well may increase retention, but it still doesn't get us any closer to learning why they've stayed in that job up to that point.

In fact, there's a lot of data on why people leave jobs and what people want from their employers; there is much less data on why people stay in jobs. In a 2009 study, John Hausknecht, of Cornell University, and Julianne Rodda, of DePaul University, sought to explore this lesser known aspect of employee retention.[11] They also attempted to see if reasons for staying varied for high performers or workers at different levels of the organization. As we addressed in Chapter 3, it's critical to target retention policies on groups of workers who yield higher returns. Retaining low-performing employees is not in the organization's best interest. Moreover, if the goal is to decrease turnover for lower-skill, hourly workers who still cost a lot to train, tactics to keep them are in all likelihood different than measures to retain all-star talent.

Hausknecht and Rodda partnered with a major leisure and hospitality organization who, like most companies, conducts annual employee engagement surveys. The study included 24,829 participants across functions and job levels, including both salaried and hourly employees.

Employees were simply asked to write their answer to the following question: "What are the top two reasons you stay employed with this company vs. the competition?" The responses were open ended so as to not lead or restrict participants. The researchers used qualitative data analysis software called ATLAS to code each response according to a list of retention factors, carefully selected based on decades of prior research on the subject. Large scale analysis of open-ended responses simply would not have been possible before the advent of big data processing tools.

The retention factors and their definitions are listed in Table 7.2.

TABLE 7.2 | RETENTION FACTORS AND DEFINITIONS FROM STUDY BY HAUSKNECHT AND RODDA

Hausknecht and Rodda scored each response under the most closely represented category.

Advancement opportunities
The amount of potential for movement to higher levels within the organization

Constituent attachments
The degree of attachment to individuals associated with the organization such as supervisor, co-workers, or customers

Extrinsic rewards
The amount of pay, benefits, or equivalents distributed in return for service

Flexible work arrangements
The nature of the work schedule or hours

Investments
Perceptions about the length of service to the organization

Job satisfaction
The degree to which individuals like their jobs

Lack of alternatives
Beliefs about the unavailability of jobs outside of the organization

Location
The proximity of the workplace relative to one's home

Non-work influences
The existence of responsibilities and commitments outside of the organization

Organizational commitment
The degree to which individuals identify with and are involved in the organization

Organizational justice
Perceptions about the fairness of reward allocations, policies and procedures, and interpersonal treatment

Organizational prestige
The degree to which the organization is perceived to be reputable and well-regarded

Source: Hausknecht, Rodda; "Targeted Employee Retention"

The researchers expected hourly employees to cite factors like extrinsic rewards and flexible work arrangements at a higher rate than managerial or professional employees, who were expected to choose relational factors like attachments to colleagues, advancement opportunities, or organizational commitment. But, as we will discuss in the next section, the results were more nuanced.

The company-wide results, including managerial, professional, and hourly employees, turned out to be quite interesting as well and should compel other organizations to run a similar analysis.

1. Job satisfaction: 51 percent

2. Extrinsic rewards: 41 percent

3. Constituent attachments: 34 percent

4. Organizational attachments: 17 percent

5. Organizational prestige: 17 percent

6. Lack of alternatives: 10 percent

7. Investments: 9 percent

8. Advancement opportunities: 8 percent

9. Location: 8 percent

10. Organizational justice: 8 percent

11. Flexible work arrangements: 7 percent

12. Non-work influences: 3 percent

Remember this is just a top-down view of one large company. There are limitations in extrapolating too far. Moreover, surveys can never get at the underlying psychological roots of an individual's decision. But in this case, for this company, it's clear job retention is a three-way race between happiness, rewards, and people. The majority of workers are not cynical in their reasoning for staying. They are not trapped by a lack of economic alternatives or only in the job for security's sake. More than half the company doesn't want to leave because they enjoy the work that they do. One-third enjoy the people they work with, which is essential to both satisfaction and retention.

However, four in ten are strongly influenced by the compensation and benefits packages, which many respondents stated were among the best in the industry. Even if satisfaction and overall engagement are more practical and efficient ways of boosting employee retention, we can't deny that the paycheck matters. But who does it matter for most?

SALARIED/PROFESSIONAL VERSUS HOURLY WORKERS

The most significant implication of the study lies in the answer to Hausknecht's and Rodda's hypothesis that there should be significant differences in what factors compel salaried and hourly workers to stay with a company. Table 7.3 shows the top five reasons for each of these groups.

TABLE 7.3 | TOP RETENTION FACTORS: HOURLY VS. SALARY

	Hourly	Salaried
1	Job Satisfaction - 53%	Job Satisfaction - 63%
2	Extrinsic Rewards - 47%	Constituent Attachments - 36%
3	Constituent Attachments - 35%	Advancement Opportunities - 30%
4	Organizational Commitment - 18%	Extrinsic Rewards - 29%
5	Lack of Alternatives/Org. Prestige - 11%	Organizational Prestige - 27%

Source: Hausknecht, Rodda; "Targeted Employee Retention"

Based on this information, a company should be able to craft engagement and retention strategies tailored to different worker classes. Compared to hourly workers, salaried workers are more inclined to stay with the organization due to perceived advancement opportunities and organizational prestige. Moreover, retention goals can be better achieved for hourly workers by staying a step ahead of the competition's wages and benefits.

In both categories, the importance of relationships and overall job satisfaction is crucial. Persistent negative interactions with managers or colleagues are a plague to retention, as we discussed earlier in the chapter. So too is the employee's enjoyment of the job itself. Naturally, much of these areas are out of HR's control. But leadership should make every effort to shape managerial strategy and on-the-job culture to ensure departments and teams get along and that the work itself is as engaging as possible.

Perhaps one of the most important findings, however, relates to why employment branding is essential to retention efforts. Hausknecht and Rodda concluded in their report:

> "One of the novel recommendations that stems directly from our research is the finding that organizational prestige shaped the decision to stay among many respondents. Whereas efforts to promote the organization's reputation or brand have been shown to influence [an] applicant's attraction to the organization during the recruitment phase, our findings show that organizational prestige also offers retention benefits for employees who are currently on the job."

For this company, salaried or professional employees are much more likely to commit to a company based on perceptions of prestige than hourly workers. Think about why this is likely the case at any organization. If you possess skills that allow you to move freely from job to job, factors besides pay and benefits will likely become more important. After all, your personal identity is in some way attached to the organization for which you work and while our professional personas aren't entirely defined by the companies we work for, they play a big role in how we are perceived and how we perceive others. It is for this reason high-performing professional workers place weight on prestige and culture when committing to an organization.

Fortunately, this is a narrative that employers can control. Employment branding is as much for retention as it is recruitment.

RETENTION PHILOSOPHIES THAT WORK

There is no silver bullet retention strategy. As we learned, employees are influenced by any number of factors to stay or leave, but there are unmistakable similarities between companies capable of retaining valued talent year after year. When you browse national or local "Best Places to Work" lists, you'll notice that many of the themes from the research presented above make an appearance. Employees are treated fairly. They feel recognized. They are engaged. They are respected. They are proud to work for their employer, and that pride often turns outward, making them the most effective employment brand marketing tool of all.

Before even considering specific tactics, HR must lay a well-researched foundation for action. If your company lists retaining top talent among its top staffing challenges, make sure it is tracking what it does well and what it does poorly in this regard, if it isn't already.

Widely-used employee attitude surveys often accomplish this, but the data gleaned has to be pegged to specific business goals. So what if worker satisfaction scores have increased eight percentage points year-over-year or surpassed an industry benchmark? In isolation, that data is only useful if you're looking to give yourself a pat on the back. Instead, take your historical survey data and measure that against turnover or productivity rates. Determine what motivates specific types of workers and how you can tangibly address employee concerns. If the employee survey is truly a helpful guide to improving talent management, the results should be positively correlated to other trends in the organization.

With that said, what are companies actually doing about retention? You'd assume most are doing *something*. After all, retention is the top staffing challenge according to senior leaders. Interestingly, a recent CareerBuilder survey found that six in ten companies have not taken any measures to strengthen retention post-recession. Fortunately, the other 40 percent appear to be on the right track. Here are the top five initiatives these companies have put into place in their efforts to retain top talent:

- ▶ Increased recognition: 46 percent

- ▶ Provided flexible work schedules: 42 percent

- ▶ Asked employees what changes they want to see and put feedback into action: 43 percent

- ▶ Increased training/learning opportunities: 36 percent

- ▶ Increased salaries: 31 percent (IT and manufacturing companies report 36 percent)

Besides the extrinsic reward of higher salaries (which again, is important up to a point) the items on this list reflect a retention philosophy centered on boosting employee engagement. Research from the Corporate Executive Board found that employees who are most committed to their organizations are 87 percent less likely to resign than those who are disengaged. They were also found to expend about 57 percent more effort.[12]

Engagement is a broad concept. Let's explore what environments contribute to the most engaged employees.

CREATING A CONSISTENT, IDENTIFIABLE EMPLOYMENT BRAND

A worker proud of her place of employment will be more reticent to leave it, as the Cornell/Depaul research indicates. Culture matters. You can't expect to have many fully engaged and satisfied employees who also don't identify with a company's mission or employment brand.

We sat down with Rick Purdy, ResCare Chief HR Officer and Tom Heetderks, vice president of talent management at ResCare, and talked about the company's continuing efforts to create an employment brand and promote a culture that resonates not only with potential recruits, but also with their existing employees. ResCare, as we learned in Chapter 5, is a leader in the workforce development space, but that's only one pillar of their human services business. They also provide extensive home care services for people of all ages, physical conditions, and cognitive disabilities. This includes professional nursing and senior care. Expanding businesses include child care and educational services, and an alternative pharmacy service designed for people with developmental and intellectual disabilities.

In short, the entirety of ResCare's business model is built on the core of values of Respect and Care. The largest segment of their nearly 50,000 person workforce is direct care, which is the fastest growing occupational group in the U.S. It is difficult, purpose-driven work, and requires compassionate, empathetic people to succeed on the job. Purdy set the agenda and is working closely with Heetderks to ensure the strategy is successful centering their employment brand on the company's mission. Heetderks reminds us that the purpose of branding extends far beyond recruitment. "We want our employment brand to be a powerful foundation not only for talent acquisition but also for many of the subsequent people initiatives that our new hires will experience," he said. "As a key part of a larger, smart retention strategy, a winning employment brand is underappreciated as a powerful way to connect with and thus retain valued employees."

Heetderks explained, the message must ring true. "Similar to consumer brands, many employment brands and campaigns are limited and temporal by design. Many times they're as fleeting as the department budgets that created them," he said. "If a company is true to the promises conveyed in the employment brand messaging, a new hire will know this soon after joining your company. On the other hand, if a company is *not* true to the promises, all current employees will respond cynically."

Heetderks is right. The recruitment promise must match on-the-job reality. This means that an organizational culture or employment brand can't be imposed on a company. It must be in some sense employee-generated—organic reflections of what workers actually feel and experience. Anything else is false advertising. And we all know false advertising breeds consumer discontent. In this case, insincerity can drive harmful turnover. This is why Purdy and his team reinforce their brand by living up to ResCare's name with their own human capital—respecting, recognizing and caring for the needs and accomplishments of their employees.

BUILDING A CULTURE OF RECOGNITION

A 2012 CareerBuilder study found that if they can't get pay, most workers want more recognition. In fact more recognition won out by a significant margin. Forty percent of workers chose recognition, followed by the simple act of setting realistic performance goals and providing training opportunities at 31 percent and 27 percent, respectively. Increased recognition is also the second ranked reason a majority of workers would prefer working for a small company (500 employees or less), according to the study.

We tend to think of recognition as major company award programs—company vacations, lifetime service awards, or "employee of the year" style programs. Those are very important, but we can't gloss over the fact that the most valuable, and often most overlooked form of recognition starts with the day-to-day experience. We saw this clearly in the data regarding manager perceptions and work flight.

In their book, *The Carrot Principle,* management experts Adrian Gostick and Chester Elton make the case for comprehensive recognition programs rooted in basic management theory.[13]

"Perks like tuition reimbursement can never take the place of a front-line supervisor who sets clear goals, communicates, builds trust, holds employees accountable, and then recognizes in an effective manner," they write. They cite a Wichita State University study that found only one in five workers felt his or her immediate manager had ever offered public recognition. Fewer than half of workers said their boss gave them a personal thank you.

More broadly, recognition on the job is about understanding the deeper needs and goals of your workers and supporting them however possible. Rick Purdy, chief human resources officer at ResCare, explained that wage rigidity is one of his toughest retention roadblocks for the company's direct care workers. Despite the critical role they play in America's health care industry, direct care workers, on average, don't make much more than the minimum wage. Because providers like ResCare are primarily paid via the Medicare and Medicaid programs, the wages of direct care workers are essentially set by the federal government. Despite this, Purdy makes it the company's goal to help workers progress, however they define it.

"We're committed to every one of our nearly 50,000 employees and want to help each of them, if they are interested, take the next step in their career," he said. "Some of our employees want to stay right where they're at. Others are looking for more and added responsibilities. They want to take advantage of the benefits of working in a company the size of ResCare." Purdy notes that each year employees collaborate with their supervisors to set goals for performance as well as personal development.

Each employee assesses his strengths and areas where he needs additional training or education to meet career goals. The plan supports and promotes professional development and achievement. "We have a passion to get better and better at career development at ResCare—we're not there yet—but we're making the investments to do an even better job with this. Ideally, we hope that each person can begin and end their career with ResCare."

We were happy to learn this isn't just rhetoric. Purdy explained that more than 30 ResCare executives and senior level employees began their careers at the company in frontline direct care or other low-paying roles.

Troy Robb is a good example. He started his career with ResCare as a van driver and direct support worker for people with developmental disabilities. Robb took on greater responsibility within group home programs, before moving into leadership roles at the state and regional levels. He is now an operations officer for the company's largest business unit, ResCare Residential Services.

We asked Purdy if this was just an anomaly. A few dozen incredible success stories notwithstanding, what about the thousands of other direct care workers? He immediately pointed us to data showing where direct care workers were employed prior to ResCare, and where they went after. Most people came from other low-paying retail and service positions, but upon leaving ResCare, one in five workers had obtained additional skills and certifications that lead to higher paying jobs in health care. Twelve percent became certified nursing assistants and 10 percent became medical assistants.

"Leaving ResCare, we see fewer going back to traditional customer service roles. We also see higher mobility for those that have enhanced their skills while here. We're encouraged to see the impact of building people's capabilities," Purdy explained. "And we'll continue investing in our talent. At the same time, we know that we've got to be even smarter to ensure that this talent stays with us."

Once a company recognizes what their employees need to thrive, it becomes equally as important to tangibly recognize superb performance. This must be done at different levels:

▶ **Frequent, small expressions of recognition.** The power of a simple thank you or good job, an occasional unplanned lunch or team social event cannot be overlooked. These small tokens of recognition are often the foundation of day-to-day job satisfaction. There are still many people who believe a paycheck is the only form of recognition that should matter to the worker, but the data and a basic understanding of psychology tell us that is not how people think. Most importantly, managers need to make sure these expressions are tied to specific work tasks the employee or employees have done well. We're all experts at gauging whether an act is sincere or simply "going through the motions."

▶ **Scheduled reward plans.** These can be anything from a quarterly bonus structure to an intradepartmental gift for above and beyond work. The key here is accountability. If managers hand out recognition like participation ribbons, the effect is lost. Expectations and parameters for these rewards must be clearly defined and always go to those deserving.

▶ **Company-wide recognition.** Career service or "employee of the year"-style awards fit the bill here. Most large companies have such programs, but the trick is to develop programs that are truly aspirational. In the next section, we'll see how companies that empower employees to innovate, and in return, recognize them for their efforts, find this is often the type of recognition that benefits a business most.

So what are the empirical results of recognition strategies? Gostick and Elton note that average turnover rate of employers with a clear reward strategy is 13 percent lower than that of organizations without one, according to a survey of 614 employers that have 3.5 million employees in total.

UNLEASHING THE LATENT INNOVATORS

Many highly skilled workers are only valuable to their companies for the expertise they bring to their day-to-day job. But that's an extremely unfortunate perspective. The role any given worker plays is often the proverbial "tip of the iceberg" when it comes to her overall potential. In the knowledge economy, it's next to impossible for an organization to stay ahead of its competition when only a handful of workers are tasked with innovation and business development. It's inefficient, stifles creativity and is antiquated in its understanding of many workers' willingness and desire to create.

As the data throughout this chapter indicates, many talented workers stay at their companies because they know there's something more the company can offer them, and vice versa. "Advancement opportunities" are not just promotions, but chances to show off latent competencies and creative ideas to improve the company as a whole.

This is why more and more companies at the front end of the knowledge economy are empowering their workers to pitch an idea and implement it. This benefits the organization's innovative capacity and will also entice key players to stick around for the next opportunity to take their ideas to the top.

One of the more popular examples seen today in the tech community is the concept of "hacking" competitions—in which employees are given an opportunity to tear apart the loose ends of a product, process, or technology and offer workable business solutions. This was popularized by Facebook, but has since spread across Silicon Valley and across the country. They're also becoming instrumental pieces of companies' employment brands. For instance, ESPN documented its "hackathon" event on the company's behind the scenes blog, and Yelp promotes theirs directly on the careers page.[14]

There's an important caveat to these types of events. Tapping into workers "intraprenuerial" abilities only works if a company is willing to embrace the possibility of failure. If workers are creatively timid due to a fear of potential consequences, the more likely they are to keep their heads down and focus on the requirements of their daily role.

When we think about why talent acquisition and human resource professionals devote so much time, heart, and energy into recruiting and developing the very best workers, witnessing examples of an employee who innovates from within and makes a lasting impact on an organization is truly the best explanation for their efforts. These proven and potential all-stars—and there are a lot of them out there—will be the core differentiator for firms in the knowledge economy.

Conclusion:
Investing in the Most Important Asset

An organization's most important asset is its people. While most business leaders would agree wholeheartedly with that sentiment, it's more difficult to determine whether or not they back it up in practice. One way of telling is by paying attention to how businesses define their workforce. Is labor merely a cost of doing business? Or is labor an investment with appreciating returns? Companies that genuinely view employees as investments will be better prepared to attract, develop, and retain the best talent.

Most importantly, such a vision is integral to achieving a company's bottom-line goals. In the knowledge economy, the depth and uniqueness of an individual's skills and strategic thinking are often the "infrastructure" that differentiates firms, which is why companies like consulting giant Deloitte invest in employee development regardless of the economic cycle. Diana O'Brien, the managing principal of Deloitte University——the firm's core learning and training program—recently told *Forbes*: "If we didn't invest in the development of our professionals, it would be akin to a manufacturer not upgrading equipment, yet still expecting improved productivity."[1] This principle isn't just true of professional services firms. After studying select major retailers for more than a decade, a researcher at MIT's Sloan School found that many of the most successful companies are able to pay their employees better than competitors and offer consistent schedules and good benefits, while simultaneously keeping prices low. How is that so? The productivity gains and increased sales revenue generated by treating retails workers well will far outpace the short-term benefits from trimming hours, freezing pay, or reducing floor coverage.[2]

The HR department is often the vanguard in the fight to make such advantageous human capital investments. Having the right data in place creates buy-in throughout an organization. At every stage of the employee life cycle, we learned how a data-driven approach can lead to a stronger workforce.

To attract the best talent pool, employers must measure the behaviors and preferences of candidates' job search, as well as understand their attitudes and perceptions of the employment brand. Because the job seeker is a consumer, the process is no different than any other strategic marketing campaign.

When recruiting tough-to-fill vacancies, the right data can identify the causes and solutions of skills shortages. Extended vacancies might be the result of regional supply-and-demand imbalances. In this case, powerful analytics tools can help recruiters identify the easiest areas to recruit and predict talent gaps several years out. Vacancies can also be the result of uncompetitive wages. The war for talent can't be won by recruiters who are outbid by competitors who know current compensation data. Talent pools can also be strengthened by developing a robust workforce planning strategy involving analysis of the projected skills mix needed years in the future, balanced with an audit of the organization's current workforce statistics—age, education, competencies, tenure, etc. Establishing and growing a multifunctional talent pipeline can reduce the time and cost of new hires and reach skilled candidates in new ways. HR managers and hiring managers should also know to what extent the applicant experience itself contributes to talent shortages. Over the past several years, according to the data referenced in Chapter 5, millions of job seekers simply abandoned applications that were too long, didn't work on a mobile device, or made them jump through unnecessary hoops. On the back end of the application process, employers often eliminate qualified candidates simply because their past titles didn't resemble the title in the job listing. Recruiting for skilled talent is tough as it is; yet many employers inadvertently make recruitment more difficult by restricting the size and quality of their talent pools.

Data analytics in HR is evolving well beyond the optimization of the recruiting process. Companies that view their existing workforces analytically can unlock the door to new efficiencies. For instance, increasing the levels of education in certain functions—specifically in sales and customer service—may help firms improve their market performance. Similarly, companies able to keep IT staffs and customer service teams together for more than five years are likely to have higher value added per employee compared to companies that do not. But those examples are just the beginning; workforce analytics can be used to leverage the full power of training and on-boarding programs, retention strategies, performance metrics, benefits and compensation plans, and everything in between. As we said at the outset, the movement toward a big data-focused HR operation will likely require new skill sets and an expansion of typical job functions, but these are necessary steps to making any HR department the strategic consulting operation so many company executives desire.

A unique set of challenges continue to loom: a tumultuous global economy, changing skills needs, shifting labor force demographics, managing global workforces, and the adoption of new technologies. When armed with the best information and approach, we have no doubt the human resources function will be critical to navigating these issues. HR will continue to change the way companies empower employment, and big data can help guide the way.

Notes

INTRODUCTION

1. IBM, What is Big Data? http://www–01.ibm.com/software/data/bigdata/

2. Josh Bersin, Big Data in HR: Why it's Here and What it Means. 2012. https://www.bersin.com/blog/post.aspx?id=574b5527-ce55–4ec6–8c45–c8f05f85162e

3. James Manyika, Michael Chui, Brad Brown, Jacques Bughin, Richard Dobbs, Charles Roxburgh, Angela Hung Byers, Big data: The next frontier for innovation, competition, and productivity, McKinsey & Company, 2011. http://www.mckinsey.com/insights/business_technology/big_data_the_next_frontier_for_innovation

CHAPTER 1

1. Joe Weisenthal, Labor Force Participation Rate Falls to Lowest Level Since September 1981. *Business Insider*, 2012. http://www.businessinsider.com/labor-force-shrinks-by–367000--participation-rate-falls-to-its-lowest-level-in–31-years–2012–9

2. CareerBuilder/Harris Interactive studies are cited throughout *The Talent Equation*. For more information about the data and survey methodology, please visit the CareerBuilder press room: http://www.careerbuilder.com/share/aboutus/pr_main.aspx

3. Jeffery Sachs, Move America's economic debate out of its time warp. *Financial Times*, 2012. http://jeffsachs.org/2012/07/move-americas-economic-debate-out-of-its-time-warp/

4. Jacob Goldstein & Lam Thuy Vo, What America Does For Work. NPR, 2012. http://www.npr.org/blogs/money/2012/03/20/149015363/what-america-does-for-work

5. Countdown to the Closing Bell, Fox Business, 2013. http://video.foxbusiness.com/v/2165570838001/warren-buffett-housing-market-is-getting-better/

6. Derek Thompson, What's the Single Best Explanation of Middle-Class Decline? *The Atlantic*, 2012. http://www.theatlantic.com/business/archive/2012/08/whats-the-single-best-explanation-for-middle-class-decline/261355/

7. James Fallows, Mr. China Comes to America, *The Atlantic*, 2012. http://www.theatlantic.com/magazine/archive/2012/12/mr-china-comes-to-america/309160/4/

8. Richard Dobbs, Anu Madgavkar, Dominic Barton, Eric Labaye, James Manyika, Charles Roxburgh, Susan Lund, & Siddarth Madhav, The world at work: Jobs, pay, and skills for 3.5 billion people, McKinsey & Company, 2012. http://www.mckinsey.com/insights/employment_and_growth/the_world_at_work

9. Anthony P. Carnevale, Nicole Smith, & Jeff Strohl, Help Wanted: Projections of Jobs and Education Requirements Through 2018, Georgetown University Center on Education and the Workforce, 2010. http://www9.georgetown.edu/grad/gppi/hpi/cew/pdfs/HelpWanted.Executive-Summary.pdf

10. BLS Employment Projections, 2010–2020. http://bls.gov/news.release/ecopro.nr0.htm

11. Prasanna Tambe & Lorin Hitt, Now IT's Personal: Offshoring and the Shifting Skill Composition of the US Information Technology Workforce. *Management Science*, April 2012, vol. 58:678–695.

12. Brad Smith, How to Reduce America's Talent Deficit. *The Wall Street Journal*, 2012. http://online.wsj.com/article/SB10000872396390443675 404578058163640361032.html

13. Emily Maltby, Small Firms Seek Skilled Workers but Can't Find Any. *The Wall Street Journal*, 2012. http://online.wsj.com/article/SB10000872396 39044484010457754913 1609451256.html

14. David Wessel, A Jobless Dilemma: What's Wrong With Fort Wayne? *The Wall Street Journal*, 2012. http://online.wsj.com/article/SB10001424127 88732331680457816 1141400688884.html

15. Pat Maio, Welding trade sees pickup in hiring despite worker shortage. U.T. San Diego, 2012. http://www.nctimes.com/business/economy-welding-trade-sees-pickup-in-hiring-despite-worker-shortage/article_0eb9618b–6196–5521–9bc6-e77fe2a87d86.html

16. Salary Guides, Robert Half International, 2013. http://www.rhi.com/salaryguides

17. Ben Casselman, Help Wanted: In Unexpected Twist, Some Skilled Jobs Go Begging. *The Wall Street Journal*, 2011. http://online.wsj.com/article/SB10001424052970203707504577010080035955166.html

18. Closing the Manufacturing Skills Gap, 2013. SHRM Executive Briefings. http://www.shrm.org/about/foundation/products/Documents/4-13%20 Skills%20Gap%20Briefing.pdf

19. Skills Gap in U.S. Manufacturing Is Less Pervasive Than Many Believe, Boston Consulting Group, 2012. http://www.bcg.com/media/pressreleasedetails.aspx?id=tcm:12-118945

20. Talent Crunch Study, CareerBuilder/Harris Interactive, 2012. http://www.careerbuilder.com/share/aboutus/pressreleasesdetail.aspx?sd=6%2F27%2 F2012&id=pr705&ed=12%2F31%2F2012

21. David Wessel, A Jobless Dilemma: What's Wrong With Fort Wayne? *The Wall Street Journal*, 2012. http://online.wsj.com/article/SB10001424127 88732331680457816 1141400688884.html

22. Catherine Rampell, With Positions to Fill, Employers Wait for Perfection. *The New York Times*, 2013. http://www.nytimes.com/2013/03/07/business/economy/despite-job-vacancies-employers-shy-away-from-hiring.html?_r=0

23. Peter Cappelli, If There's a Gap, Blame It on the Employer. *The New York Times*, 2012. http://www.nytimes.com/roomfordebate/ 2012/07/09/does-a-skills-gap-contribute-to-unemployment/if-theres-a-skills-gap-blame-it-on-the-employer

24. Aysegul Sahin, Joseph Song, Giorio Topa, & Giovanni L.Violante, Mismatch Unemployment. Federal Reserve Bank of New York, 2012. http://www.newyorkfed.org/research/economists/sahin/USmismatch.pdf

25. "CareerBuilder and Harris Interactive Q2 2012 Employer Survey."

26. U.S. Manufacturing in Context. Manufacturing.gov. http://www.manufacturing.gov/mfg_in_context. June 2012.

27. Bureau of Economic Analysis, Industry-by-Industry Total Requirements Table.

28. Enrico Moretti, *The New Geography of Jobs*. Boston: Houghton Mifflin Harcourt, 2012.

CHAPTER 2

1. *The Writings of Thomas Jefferson* (1861). Editor H.A. Washington. New York : H.W. Derby.

2. Address to the People of Sangamon County. *The Writings of Abraham Lincoln, Volume 1*. http://www.classicreader.com/book/3237/5/

3. Franklin D. Roosevelt: "Message for American Education Week", September 27, 1938. The American Presidency Project. http://www.presidency.ucsb.edu/ws/?

4. Pew Research, Is College Worth It? 2011. http://www.pewsocialtrends.org/2011/05/15/is-college-worth-it/

5. Lee Laurence, Bachelor's degree: Has it lost its edge and its value? *The Christian Science Monitor*, 2012. http://www.csmonitor.com/

The-Culture/Family/2012/0617/Bachelor-s-degree-Has-it-lost-its-edge-and-its-value

6. Charles Murray, Narrowing the New Class Divide, *The New York Times*, 2012. http://www.nytimes.com/2012/03/08/opinion/reforms-for-the-new-upper-class.html?_r=0

7. The Condition of Education. *National Center for Education Statistics*, May 2013. http://nces.ed.gov/pubs2013/2013037.pdf

8. Jonathan Rothewell, Education, Job Openings, and Unemployment in Metropolitan America, Metropolitan Policy Program, Brookings Institution, 2012. http://www.brookings.edu/~/media/Research/Files/Papers/2012/8/29%20education%20gap%20rothwell/29%20education%20gap%20rothwell.pdf

9. Michael Greenstone & Adam Looney, College: Expensive, but a smart choice, *Los Angeles Times*, 2011. http://articles.latimes.com/2011/aug/15/opinion/la-oe-looney-greenstone-is-college-wo20110815

10. BLS, Current Population Survey, Education Pays, 2012. http://www.bls.gov/emp/ep_chart_001.htm

11. Jonathan James, The College Wage Premium, Federal Reserve Bank of Cleveland, 2012. http://www.clevelandfed.org/research/commentary/2012/2012–10.cfm

12. Tiffany Julian, Work–Life Earnings by Field of Degree and Occupation for People With a Bachelor's Degree: 2011, 2012. http://www.census.gov/prod/2012pubs/acsbr11–04.pdf

13. Federal Reserve Bank of Cleveland; ibid.

14. Anthony P. Carnevale, Jeff Strohl, & Michelle Melton, What's it Worth? The economic value of college majors, Georgetown University Center on Education and the Workforce, 2011. http://cew.georgetown.edu/whatsitworth/

15. Michelle Jamrisko & Illan Kolet, "Cost of College Degree in U.S. Soars 12 Fold: Chart of the Day." Bloomberg.com. August 15, 2012. http://www.bloomberg.com/news/2012-08-15/cost-of-college-degree-in-u-s-soars-12-fold-chart-of-the-day.html

16. Andrew Martin, Degrees of Debt: A Generation Hobbled by the Soaring Cost of College, *The New York Times*, 2012. http://www.nytimes.com/2012/05/13/business/student-loans-weighing-down-a-generation-with-heavy-debt.html?pagewanted=all&_r=0

17. Nathan Koppel & Douglas Belkin, Texas Pushes $10,000 Degree, *The Wall Street Journal*, 2012. http://online.wsj.com/article/SB10000872396390443493304578039040237714224.html

18. Senator Tom Harkin, 8 Ideas to Improve Higher Education: Make College Costs More Transparent, *Time*, 2012. http://ideas.time.com/2012/10/18/8-ideas-to-improve-higher-education/slide/make-college-costs-more-transparent/

19. Mary Beth Marklein, College may never be the same, *USA Today*, 2012. http://usatoday30.usatoday.com/news/nation/story/2012/09/12/college-may-never-be-the-same/57752972/1

20. Tony Hsieh: Redefining Zappos' Business Model, *Bloomberg Businessweek*, May 27, 2010. http://www.businessweek.com/magazine/content/10_23/b4181088591033.htm

21. Prasanna Tambe, Lorin Hitt, & Erik Brynjolfsson, The Price and Quantity of IT-Related Intangible Capital, December 6, 2011. *ICIS 2011 Proceedings*. Paper 16. http://aisel.aisnet.org/icis2011/proceedings/economicvalueIS/16

CHAPTER 3

1. Kyle Kennedy, Public's Clatyon Hollis Retiring After 40 Years, *The Ledger*, 2012. http://www.theledger.com/article/20121102/NEWS/121109836

2. AARP, Centegra Health System and John Deere Once Again Listed as AARP's Best Employers for Workers Over 50, *PR Newswire*, 2012. http://www.prnewswire.com/news-releases/centegra-health-system-and-john-deere-once-again-listed-as-aarps-best-employers-for-workers-over–50–56272017.html

3. M.J. Stephey, A Brief History of Tenure, *Time*, 2008. http://www.time.com/time/nation/article/0,8599,1859505,00.html

4. Bureau of Labor Statistics, Employee Tenure in September 18, 2012. http://www.bls.gov/news.release/pdf/tenure.pdf

5. CareerBuilder, Generational Differences in Work Styles, Communication and Changing Jobs, 2012. http://www.careerbuilder.com/share/aboutus/pressreleasesdetail.aspx?sd=9%2f13%2f2012&siteid=cbpr&sc_cmp1=cb_pr715_&id=pr715&ed=12%2f31%2f2012

6. Susan Hall, Employee Tenure: 2–3 Years and Gone? *IT Business Edge*, 2011. http://www.itbusinessedge.com/cm/blogs/hall/employee-tenure–2–3-years-and-gone/?cs=47811

7. Jim Meyerle, Big Data Debunks View That Job-Hoppers Make Bad Hires. *Forbes*, 2012. http://www.forbes.com/sites/ciocentral/2012/11/04/big-data-debunks-view-that-job-hoppers-make-bad-hires/

8. Penelope Trunk, Why Job Hoppers Make the Best Employees, CBS MoneyWatch, 2010. http://www.cbsnews.com/8301–505125_162–45040110/why-job-hoppers-make-the-best-employees/

9. Mark Suster, Never Hire Job Hoppers. Never. They Make Terrible Employees, *Business Insider*, 2010. http://www.businessinsider.com/mark-suster-never-hire-job-hoppers-never-they-make-terrible-employees–2010–4

10. Bureau of Labor Statistics, Number of Jobs Held, Labor Market Activity, and Earnings Growth Among the Youngest Baby Boomers: Results from a Longitudinal Survey Summary, 2012. http://www.bls.gov/news.release/nlsoy.nr0.htm

11. Prasanna Tambe & Lorin M. Hitt, Job Hopping, Information Technology Spillovers, and Productivity Growth (January 25, 2013). *Management Science*, Forthcoming. Available at SSRN: http://ssrn.com/abstract=1302637

CHAPTER 4

1. Office of the Press Secretary, Fact Sheet: President Obama's Commitment to Employing America's Veterans, 2011. http://www.whitehouse.gov/

the-press-office/2011/08/05/fact-sheet-president-obama-s-commitment-employing-america-s-veterans

2. Leo Shane, III, Mandatory reverse boot camp will prepare troops to leave military, *Stars and Stripes*, 2012. http://www.stripes.com/news/us/mandatory-reverse-boot-camp-will-prepare-troops-to-leave-military–1.183688

3. Bureau of Labor Statistics, Employment Situation of Veterans—2012. http://www.bls.gov/news.release/vet.nr0.htm

4. Nancy Goldstein & Karen Mellen, Accenture Study Finds U.S. Workers Under Pressure to Improve Skills, But Need More Support from Employers, *Accenture Newsroom*, 2012. http://newsroom.accenture.com/news/accenture-study-finds-us-workers-under-pressure-to-improve-skills-but-need-more-support-from-employers.print

5. Josh Bersin, Growing Mismatch between Education and the Needs of Business, 2012. http://www.linkedin.com/today/post/article/20121210001305–131079-want-a-job-get-training-anywhere?trk=mp-edit-rr-posts

6. Peter Cappelli, *Why Good People Can't Get Jobs: The Skills Gap and What Companies Can Do about It*, Philadelphia, PA: Wharton Digital, 2012.

7. Mark Lowenstein & James Spletzer, Dividing the costs and returns to general training, *Highbeam Business*, 1998. http://business.highbeam.com/437018/article–1G1–20471086/dividing-costs-and-returns-general-training

8. Motoko Rich, Federal Funds to Train the Jobless Are Drying Up, *The New York Times*, 2012. http://www.nytimes.com/2012/04/09/business/economy/federal-funds-to-train-jobless-are-drying-up.html

9. Jon Newberry, Applications for Ohio worker training vouchers going fast, *Cincinnati Business Courier*, 2013. http://www.bizjournals.com/cincinnati/blog/2013/01/applications-for-ohio-worker-training.html

10. Amanda McGrory-Dixon, Expert: Jobs bill makes sense for long-term unemployed, *Benefitspro*, 2011. http://www.benefitspro.com/2011/09/14/expert-jobs-bill-makes-sense-for-long-term-unemployed/

11. David Rohde, The Anti-Walmart, *Reuters*, 2012. http://blogs.reuters.com/david-rohde/2012/03/22/the-anti%E2%80%93walmart/

12. Opportunity Finance Network. http://opportunityfinance.net/about/

13. Steve Wexler, Cisco Addresses Broadening Data Center Skills Gap, *IT Trends & Analysis*, 2012. http://it-tna.com/2012/11/20/cisco-addresses-broadening-data-center-skills-gap/

14. New Tech City, Teaching a New Generation of Coders and Web Developers, WNYC, 2012. http://www.wnyc.org/shows/newtechcity/2012/sep/11/

15. Todd Bishop, Geek of the Week: Kevin Wang is putting computer scientists into high schools, *GeekWire*, 2012. http://www.geekwire.com/2012/kevin-wang/

16. Richard Branson, Employing more ex-offenders. Virgin.com, 2011. http://www.virgin.com/richard-branson/blog/employing-more-ex-offenders

17. Bank of America, Working on Bikes to Break the Cycle of Poverty, 2011. http://about.bankofamerica.com/en-us/partnering-locally/new-door-ventures.html#fbid=bpLEUOEaZBZ

18. Mike Collins, The Kind Of Training You Really Need, Manufacturing. net, 2013. http://www.manufacturing.net/articles/2013/01/the-kind-of-training-you-really-need

CHAPTER 5

1. Adapted from CareerBuilder Employment Branding E-Book: http://www.careerbuilder.com/JobPoster/Resources/page.aspx?pagever=ReportsAndeBooks

2. Dr. John Sullivan, Revelation—Your Employer Brand Is No Longer Owned by Your Firm, *ERE*, 2009. http://www.ere.net/2009/10/19/revelation-%E2%80%93-your-employer-brand-is-no-longer-owned-by-your-firm/

3. SilkRoad, Recruitment Marketing Effectiveness: Meaningful Metrics Straight From the Source, 2012. http://pages.silkroad.com/Source-of-Hire.html?campaign=70160000000XcCj

4. Lauren Weber, Your Resume vs. Oblivion. *The Wall Street Journal*, 2012. http://online.wsj.com/article/SB10001424052970204624204577178941034941330.html

5. Karen O'Leonard, The Talent Acquisition Factbook 2011, *Bersin & Associates Executive Summary v.1.0*, 2011. http://marketing.bersin.com/rs/bersin/images/111111_ES_TAFB-ExecSumm_KOL.pdf

CHAPTER 6

1. For a summary on this history, read: Richard M. Vosburgh, The Evolution of HR: Developing HR as an Internal Consulting Organization, *Human Resource Planning Society*, 2007. http://c.ymcdn.com/sites/www.hrps.org/resource/resmgr/p_s_article_preview/hrps_issue30.3_evolutionofhr.pdf

2. Clint Boulton, For HR, the Cloud Is Where It's At, *CIO Journal*, 2012. http://blogs.wsj.com/cio/2012/09/19/for-hr-the-cloud-is-where-its-at/

3. Andrew Arno & Robert Metzger, HR Technology Insights, William Blair, 2012. http://williamblair.com/~/media/downloads/emarketing/2012/ib/hr_technology_2012_08.pdf?mkt_tok=3RkMMJWWfF9wsRokuKrBZKXonjHpfsX77+0kW7Hr08Yy0EZ5VunJEUWy2YQBTNQhcOuuEwcWGog81wVUFumUcYJM+/xP

4. Erik Brynjolfsson, Lorin M. Hitt, & Heekyung Hellen Kim, Strength in Numbers: How Does Data-Driven Decision-making Affect Firm Performance? (April 22, 2011). Available at SSRN: http://ssrn.com/abstract=1819486

5. Sinan Aral, Erik Brynjolfsson, & Lynn Wu, Three-Way Complementarities: Performance Pay, HR Analytics and Information Technology, *Management Science*, May 2012, Vol. 58 Issue 5, p. 913. Available at SSRN: http://ssrn.com/abstract=1665945

6. Claire Schooley, Recruitment Aligns With Talent Management, *Forrester*, March 2, 2011. http://webprod.forrester.com/Recruitment+Aligns+Wit h+Talent+Management/-/E-RES58159?objectid=RES58159

7. Sara Cicero, Cisco's VNI Forecast Projects the Internet Will Be Four Times as Large in Four Years, Cisco Press Room, 2012. http://newsroom. cisco.com/press-release-content?articleId=888280

8. IDC Press Release, 2011. http://www.idc.com/about/viewpressrelease.jsp? containerId=prUS22689111&sectionId=null&elementId=null&pageType =SYNOPSIS#.UVohehxllYk

9. Cisco. Ibid.

10. Walker Sands Communications, Press Room Study Finds Mobile Traffic Quadrupled In Last Two Years, 2013. http://www.walkersands.com/ quarterlymobiletraffic

11. Nielsen Press Room, Watching TV Don't Forget Your Smartphone, Tablet, 2012. http://blog.nielsen.com/nielsenwire/consumer/watching-tv-dont-forget-your-smartphone-tablet/

12. eMarketer, The Future of Smart Mobile Devices, 2011. http://www. emarketer.com/Article/Future-of-Smart-Mobile-Devices/1008228

13. Paul Davidson, Old tech deters job seekers. *USA Today*, March 6, 2013.

CHAPTER 7

1. Joseph Walker, Meet the New Boss: Big Data, *Wall Street Journal*, 2012. http://online.wsj.com/article/SB100008723963904438903045780062520 19616768.html

2. KPMG, Rethinking Human Resource in a Changing World, 2012. http:// www.kpmg.com/global/en/issuesandinsights/articlespublications/hr-transformations-survey/pages/default.aspx

3. KPMG. Ibid.

4. Bureau of Labor Statistics, Job Openings and Labor Turnover Survey, 2012. http://data.bls.gov/timeseries/JTS00000000QUR

5. Boris Groysberg, *Chasing Stars: The Myth of Talent and the Portability of Performance*, Princeton, NJ: Princeton University Press, 2010.

6. Carmen Nobel, Chasing Stars: Why the Mighty Red Sox Struck Out, *Harvard Business School*, 2011. http://hbswk.hbs.edu/item/6852.html

7. Marie Gendron, Keys to Retaining Your Best Managers in a Tight Job Market, *Harvard Management Update*, vol. 3, no. 6, June 15, 1998, pp. 1-4.

8. Thad Peterson, Why Employees Leave: Q&A With Author Leigh Branham, *Globoforce*, 2012. http://www.globoforce.com/gfblog/2012/why-employees-leave-qa-with-author-leigh-branham/

9. John E. Sheridan, Organizational Culture and Employee Retention. *The Academy of Mangement Journal*, Vol. 35, No. 5 (December 1992), pp. 1036–1056.

10. R.P. Steel, R.W. Griffeth, & P.W. Hom, Practical retention policy for the practical manager. Academy of Management Executive, 2002. Vol. 16, 149-162.

11. J.P. Hausknecht, J.M. Rodda, & M.J. Howard, Targeted employee retention: Performance-based and job-related differences in reported reasons for staying. *Human Resource Management*, 48, 269–288, 2009. http://digitalcommons.ilr.cornell.edu/articles/140

12. Corporate Executive Board, The Role of Employee Engagement in the Return to Growth, *Bloomberg Businessweek*, 2010. http://www.businessweek.com/managing/content/aug2010/ca20100813_586946.htm

13. Adrian Gostick & Chester Elston, *The Carrot Principle*, Free Press, 2007.

14. Hope Gurion, 4 Ways Leading Companies Attract Top Tech Talent, *Business Insider*, 2012. http://www.businessinsider.com/4-ways-leading-companies-attract-top-tech-talent–2012–5#ixzz2KyId9AkO

CONCLUSION

1. Lisa Quast, Want Your Company To Succeed In The Future? Invest In Employee Skills Training Like Deloitte LLP, *Forbes*, 2012. http://www.

forbes.com/sites/lisaquast/2012/05/14/want-your-company-to-succeed-in-the-future-invest-in-employee-skills-training-like-deloitte-llp/

2. Zeynep Ton, Why "Good Jobs" Are Good for Retailers, *Harvard Business Review*, 2012. http://hbr.org/2012/01/why-good-jobs-are-good-for-retailers

Index

A

AT&T, 34–35, 89, 107–108
    Academy for Software
        Engineering, 108
    advancement opportunities,
        127–128, 187–188, 202
    advertisements to communicate
        an employer brand, 123
age. *See also* Millenials
    and percent of veterans
        unemployed, 81
    tenure and, 57–58, 63–67
AIG, 113, 114, 116–120, 143–146,
    168–169
American Welding Society, 18–19
Anita Borg Memorial Scholarship,
    108
applicant tracking system (ATS),
    129–130, 144, 155
Arno, Andrew, 150
associates degree employment
    opportunities, 37
Atlas Van Lines, 95
at-risk youth, workforce preparedness
    programs, 109–110

B

baby boomers and job tenure, 67
bachelor's degree. *See* college
    education
Bank of America Foundation,
    109–110
Beckler, Melissa, 139, 144
Bersin, Josh, xi
Bertelli, Heidi, 155–157, 159,
    160, 161
Bloomberg, Michael, 73
blue-collar jobs, 18–19, 22
Branham, Leigh, 185
Branson, Richard, 108–109
Broussard, Bruce, 82
Buffett, Warren, 7
Bugala, Julie, 34
business services, job growth,
    12–13

C

candidate application experience
    applicant dropouts, 114–115, 118,
        143–144, 160–161, 172
    the bottom line and the, 116–120

candidate application experience
(*Cont.*)
communication and the
at AIG, 119–120
e-mail notifications, targeted,
161–162
employer brand, 131–134
at Nemours Foundation, 144–145
notification systems for,
116–117, 145
post-application, 130–134
improvements suggested, 116–119
negative, effects of, 114–120
Nemours Foundation, 137–146
recruiters and the, 134–137
summary overview, 209
time required to complete, results of,
114–115, 118, 160–161, 172
candidates, prospective. *See also*
recruitment
applicants per available positions,
128–130
cost per hire, 129, 154, 175
employer brand, communicating
to, 123–124
job titles, ability to translate, 157–158
Millenials, 128
reasons for applying, 125–128
resources used, 122
screening process, 114–115,
129–130, 175–177
search engines, use of, 156–159
Cappelli, Peter, 26–27, 92
career centers to communicate an
employer brand, 123

career path strategy, 77–78
Carnevale, Anthony, 14
The Carrot Principle (Gostick &
Elton), 201
Chasing Stars (Groysberg), 182
ChicagoNEXT, 73
Cisco, 107
college education. *See also* educational
attainment
affordability, 35–36, 108
employment opportunities and,
36–38, 46–48
gender and a, 36
median earnings by major,
40–41
percent earning a, growth in, 36
relevance of, 32–33
Collins, Mike, 110
compensation. *See also* earnings
potential
educational attainment and, 38–41
for length of service, 76–77
recruitment and, 126–128
retention and, 184–186
skills gap effect on, 21–23, 26–27
consumer brand-employer brand
link, 120
continuing education, 54, 93–94
Cosey, Daniel, 104
customer service workers
education and job opportunities,
50–52
growth in jobs for, 13
tenure and market performance,
70–71

D

democracy, education's impact on, 31–32

dropout prevention
applicants, 114–115, 118, 143–144, 160–161, 172
high-school students, 34–35

E

earnings potential. *See also* compensation
cost of education vs., 41–43
educational attainment and, 38–41
by occupation, 40–41, 48–50

economy, multiplier effect on the, 27–29, 38

education
as an absolute good, 31–35
cost of, 41–43
democracy, importance to, 31–32
online, 42–43

educational attainment
career preparedness and, 32
earnings potential and, 38–43
employers' views on, 46–48
employment opportunities by level of, 36–38, 46–48
gender and, 36
growth in levels of, 36
job functions impacted by, 48–56
market performance, impact on, 43–44, 47, 50–56

multiplier effect, economic impact, 38
unemployment rates by, 37

education gap, threat of, 13–15

education sector jobs, 10–11

Elkin, Noah, 169

Elton, Chester, 201, 204

Emanuel, Rahm, 73

employees, communicating an employer brand, 123

employer brand
communicating an, 123–124, 131–134
consumer brand link, 120
foundation of the, 121–124
function of, 113
job seekers, importance to, 114, 126–127
Nemours Foundation, 138–144
retention and, 195–196, 199–200

employers empowering employment, 106–110

entrepreneurs
intraprenuerial opportunities, 204
job creation, 107

ESPN, 205

ex-offenders, employing, 109

F

Facebook, 204

Fallows, James, 11–12

Farrugia, Marc, 172

Ferguson, Jim, 110

Frutiger, Gordon, 113, 114, 116–117, 120, 143, 168

G

Gates, Bill, 56
gender
  educational attainment and, 36
  tenure and, 62
geography of jobs, 2, 24, 72–73,
    126, 169
globalization
  effect on job creation, 10–11
  job skill needs, effect on, 16–17
Google, 108
Gostick, Adrian, 201, 204
government employees, tenure for,
    62–63
Great Recession era
  applicants reasons for applying,
    changes in, 125
  job creation, pre- and post-
    recession, 1–2, 8–13, 188–189
  labor market changes in, 6, 11
  tenure, effect on, 61, 180
  unemployment statistics, 28, 81, 84
Groysberg, Boris, 182–183

H

Haas, Carleen, 82, 87
Harkin, Tom, 42
Hausknecht, John, 192–195
health care workers
  job creation, pre- and post-
    recession, 10–11
  Nemours Foundation example,
    137–146
  Sunrise Senior Living example,
    155–162

Heetderks, Tom, 199–200
higher education jobs, 13–15
high-school education or less
  earnings potential, 39
  employment opportunities, 37,
    46–48
high-school students. *See also* youth
    workforce preparedness
    programs
  dropout prevention, 34–35
  high-tech preparedness programs,
    107–108
  at-risk youth workforce
    preparedness programs,
    109–110
high-tech workers. *See also* IT
    workers
  demand for, xi, 3, 12–15
  efficiently connecting to,
    159–161
  hybrid skills set for, 16–19, 35
  multiplier effect, economic
    impact, 28
  wage pressure and vacancy rates,
    21–23
  workforce preparedness programs
    for, 107–108
hiring
  applicants per available positions,
    128–130
  cost per hire, 129, 154, 175
  data-driven approach, 175–176
  tax incentives to increase, 82, 103
  time requirements, reducing, 153
Hollis, Clayton, Jr., 57

homeless population workforce
    preparedness programs,
    109–110
housing market, employment and
    turnaround in the, 6, 7
Hsieh, Tony, 51
Hubbard, A. J., 88
Humana's veterans hiring initiative,
    82–83, 85–90
human capital management (HCM)
    technology, ix–xi, 150–151
human resources
    data-focused, benefits of, 209
    historically vs. present-day
        perceptions of, 149–150
human resources technology
    solutions. *See also* recruitment
    strategies, digital/
    technological
    applicant tracking system (ATS),
        129–130, 144, 155
    HCM technology, ix–xi, 150–151
    present-day, 150
    recruitment analytic tools, need
        for, 151
hybrid skills sets, 16–19, 35

I
IBM, ix
Incumbent Workforce Training
    Voucher Program (Ohio), 95
IT workers. *See also* high-tech
    workers
    compensation, 22
    demand for, 12–13, 107–108

education and job opportunities,
    53–56
hacking competitions, 204–205
intraprenuerial opportunities,
    204–205
tenure and market performance,
    71–73
training programs for, 104–105,
    107
wage pressure and vacancy rates,
    21–22

J
Jefferson, Thomas, 31
Jesuthasan, Ravin, 103
job creation, pre- and post-recession,
    1–2, 8–13, 188–189. *See also*
    specific industries; specific jobs
job hopping, 63–66
job matching, 156–159
job opportunities. *See also specific*
    industries; specific jobs
    educational attainment and, 13–15,
        36–38, 46–56
    employment gaps and, 101–103
    ex-offenders, 109
    growth predicted, 13–15
    by industry, changes in (1972-2012),
        6–7
    post-recession, 1–2
    pre- and post-recession job
        creation, 1–2, 8–13, 188–189
JOBS (Jump Start Our Business
    Startups) Act, 103
job satisfaction, quits rate and, 186

job seekers. *See* candidates, prospective

job vacancies
cost of, 4–5
by function, 19–21
possible reasons for, 26–27
skills gap effect on, 23–25
time to fill, 25
wage pressure and, 21–23

John Deere, tenure rates at, 57–58

K

Kmetz, Marilyn, 145

L

Learning Institute for Growth of High Technology (L.I.G.H.T.), 110
Lewis, Michael, x
Lincoln, Abraham, 31–32
Lowenstein, Mark, 94
loyalty, 57–58

M

management
demand for, xi
education and job opportunities, 52–54
tenure and market performance, 75–76

manufacturing sector
job openings, growth in, 28
multiplier effect, economic impact, 28–29

pre- and post-recession, 11–12
skills gap and the, 22–23
tenure and market performance, 75
training programs, 110
wage pressure and vacancy rates, 22–23

market performance
educational attainment and, 43–44, 47, 50–56
tenure and, 67–76

master's degrees, growth in numbers of, 36

McCallister, Mike, 82

McKinsey Global Institute, xi

media, using to communicate an employer brand, 123

Meharg, Ron, 99, 105

Metzger, Robert, 150

Microsoft's veteran training programs, 89

Millenials, 63–64, 128. *See also* age

Moneyball (film), x

Moneyball (Lewis), x

MOOC (massive online open courses), 42–43

Moretti, Enrico, 28, 29

multiplier effect, economic impact, 27–29, 38

Murray, Charles, 33

Musil, Caryn McTighe, 32–33

N

Nemours Foundation, 137–146

New Door, 109–110

The New Geography of Jobs
(Moretti), 28
Newmaster, Tom, 166

O
Oakland A's, x
Obama, Barack, 81
O'Brien, Diana, 207
off-shoring, 11, 16–17
online education, 42–43
Opportunity Finance Network
(OFN), 107
organizational culture and voluntary
quits, 190

P
Penn United Technologies, 110
performance vs. tenure, 76–80
Perry, Rick, 42
personality screening tests, 175–176
press releases to communicate an
employer brand, 123
Proctor & Gamble Inc., 129
productivity
HCM technology and, 151
tenure and, 67–70, 75
training and, 94
professional services, post-recession
job growth, 12–13
Purdy, Rick, 199–200, 201–202

R
race and educational attainment, 36
Rath, Diane, 97–98

recruitment. *See also* candidates,
prospective; recruitment
strategies, digital/technological
candidate perceptions in, 134–137
from the competition, 181–182
continuous recruitment strategy,
26, 152–155, 159
employer brand, importance to, 113
resources for, 123
summary overview, 207–209
of veterans, 86–88
recruitment applications market,
financial value of, 151
recruitment strategies, digital/
technological. *See also*
recruitment
advantages of, 156–162
data-driven approach, present-day
use of, 152
e-mail notifications, targeted,
161–162, 172
mobile technology, 152–153,
169–173
search-engine optimized job
listings, 156–160
supply and demand data, accessing
and using, 162–169
Talent Networks, 154–155,
158–161
Re-employment Initiative
(CareerBuilder), 101,
103–104
ResCare, 97–99, 199–202
resumes, 102–103, 114

retention
  challenge of, 178–183
  training and, 83–84, 94, 106
retention strategies
  advancement opportunities,
    187–188, 202
  cited by employees, 191
  compensation, 184–186
  employer branding, 195–196,
    199–200
  engagement, 198
  hiring systems, automated, 175–176
  intraprenuerial opportunities, 204
  job satisfaction, 186
  personal and professional
    development, 201–202
  recognition, 200–204
  for salaried/professional vs. hourly
    workers, 195–197
  screening tools, data-driven,
    175–177
  voluntary quits, looking at, 184–190
Rhode, David, 106
Robb, Troy, 202
Robinson, Sharee, 99–100, 105
Robison, Hank, 28–29
Rodda, Julianne, 192–195
Roosevelt, Franklin D., 32
Rowan, Lisa, 150
Ryles, Ricky, 100, 105

S
Sachs, Jeffery, 4
sales workforce, 13, 48–50, 74–75

scholarships, 108
*The 7 Hidden Reasons Employees
  Leave* (Branham), 185
SFMade, 12
Sheridan, John, 190
Silva, Matt, 100, 105
Sirkin, Harold, 22–23
skills acquisition. *See* training
skills gap, 2–3, 13–15, 20–29
small businesses
  percent of all employed workers,
    107
  training programs, 92
  workforce service centers and, 97
Smith, Brad, 18
social media to communicate an
    employer brand, 123
soft skills, 17
Spletzer, James, 94
Stakelum, Kevin, 82, 86
Starbucks, 107, 129
strategic workers, hybrid skills set for,
    16–19, 35
Sullivan, John, 124
Sunrise Senior Living, 155–162
supervisor relationship and quits
    rate, 186
Suster, Mark, 66

T
talent mismatch, 5, 18–19, 27–28
Talent Networks, 153–156, 158–160
tax incentives to increase hiring,
    82, 103

Technology Education and Literacy in Schools (TEALS), 108
temp jobs, growth in, 13
tenure
  age and, 57–58, 63–67
  average length of, 59–61
  customer service workers, 70–71
  gender and, 62
  increases in, 60–62, 67, 75–76
  IT workers and, 71–73
  at John Deere, 57–58
  management and, 75–76
  manufacturing workers and, 75
  market performance and, 67–76
  pre-recession and recovery, 161, 180
  private vs. public sector, 62–63
  productivity and, 67–70, 75
  rewarding length of service, 76–77
  sales workers and, 74–75
  term, derivation and present-day use, 58–59
Terry-Tharp, Jennifer, 34
Thompson, Derek, 10
Thrun, Sebastian, 42
training
  benefits of, 94
  closing the skills gap, 26–27
  cost per hire, 175
  IT workers, 104–105, 107
  the long-term unemployed, 3–4, 99–106
  new hires, 90–94
  productivity and, 94

  retention and, 83–84, 94, 106
  veterans, 82–83, 85–90
training programs
  company-provided, 34–35, 90–92
  funds available for, 91–92, 95–96
  manufacturing sector, 110
  need for, 25
  recruitment and, 128
  workforce service centers, 97–99
  for youth, 96
Trunk, Penelope, 66
turnover. *See* retention

U
unemployed workers
  long-term
    re-skilling and re-employing, 3–4, 99–106
    statistics, 3, 101
    tax credits for hiring, 82
  rates by education attainment, 37–38
  statistics, 2, 3, 28, 81, 101
  veterans, 81–83, 85–90

V
value add, tenure and, 70–76
veterans hiring initiative (Humana), 82–83, 85–90
veteran unemployment, 81–83, 85–90
vocational education, decline in, 18–19, 98, 110

voluntary quits. *See also* retention
 strategies
 growth in, 180–181
 reasons given for, 184–190

W

Walker, Joseph, 175
Walmart, 89
Wang, Kevin, 108
Weber, Lauren, 129
Wegmans, 106
welders, need for, 18–19
Wittes, Rob, 103–104
women
 labor force participation,
  62, 108
 tenure for, 62–63
Wood, Chris, 100, 105
workforce development grants,
 109–110

workforce preparedness programs
 for high-school high-tech workers,
  107–108
 at-risk youth, 109–110
 youth targeted, funding, 96
workforce service centers, 97–99
workplace proximity, importance of,
  2, 24, 72–73, 126, 169, 193

X

Xerox Corp., 175

Y

Yelp, 205
youth workforce preparedness
 programs, 96, 109–110.
  See also high-school students

Z

Zappos, 51

About the Authors

Matt Ferguson is the president and CEO of CareerBuilder, the global leader in human capital solutions. Ferguson took CareerBuilder to the number one position in the online recruitment industry within five years. Under his direction, CareerBuilder continues to outpace competitors in traffic, revenue, and technology innovation, and is quickly expanding its global footprint with a presence in more than 60 countries worldwide. He set into motion an evolution that has taken CareerBuilder beyond being the largest job board in the nation to a company that offers a wide range of talent intelligence and consulting services, targeted advertising, and recruitment support.

Working with the nation's top employers on a daily basis, Ferguson is often called upon to provide insights on emerging trends, the impact of the economy on the job outlook, and advice for job seekers. He has appeared on CNBC Squawk Box, ABC World News, CBS Evening News, Bloomberg TV, the TODAY Show, FOX Your World with Neil Cavuto, Nightly Business Report, and CNN Money, among others. He was named to Crain's Chicago Business "40 Under 40" and ranked in the top ten list of Glassdoor.com's "Highest Rated CEOs."

Ferguson first joined the company following CareerBuilder's acquisition of Headhunter.net, where he had been serving as senior vice president of business development. Ferguson holds a master's in business administration from the University of Chicago and a law degree from Northwestern University.

Lorin M. Hitt is a professor of Operations and Information Management (OPIM) at the University of Pennsylvania, Wharton School. He is currently a member of the Information Strategy and Economics Group (ISE) and a senior fellow of the Wharton Financial Institutions Center. His current research is on the relationship of organizational and strategic factors to the value of IT investments, the design of IT outsourcing agreements, the economics of IT labor, the nature of competition in electronic markets, the effects of online distribution on customer behavior, and methods for evaluating IT investments.

His research and teaching have earned numerous awards including the 1996 Best Academic Contribution to MIS Quarterly, Best Paper and Best Theme Paper at the 1994 International Conference on Information Systems, the 1999 Best Paper in IS Economics from the Workshop on Information Systems and Economics, nine Wharton Excellence in Teaching Awards, the David Hauck Award for undergraduate teaching at Wharton, and the Lindback Award for Distinguished Teaching at the University of Pennsylvania. His work has appeared in a variety of academic journals including the *Brookings Papers on Economic Activity*, the *Quarterly Journal of Economics*, the *Journal of Economic Perspectives*, *Management Science*, and *Information Systems Research*. He received his PhD in Management from the MIT Sloan School of Management, and ScB and ScM degrees in Electrical Engineering from Brown University.

Prasanna Tambe is an assistant professor of Information, Operations, and Management Sciences at the New York University Stern School of Business. His research interests include the economics of IT labor and how technological change has affected labor markets. In his recent papers, professor Tambe has focused on the effects of offshoring on IT skill demand in US firms and the importance of IT labor mobility for spreading IT-enabled practices among firms. His research has been published in Management Science, Information Systems Research,

Communications of the ACM, and Information Economics and Policy, and has been mentioned in press outlets including CNBC, The Wall Street Journal, and Forbes.

Professor Tambe received his SB and M. Eng. in Electrical Engineering and Computer Science from the Massachusetts Institute of Technology and his PhD in Managerial Science and Applied Economics from the Wharton School of the University of Pennsylvania.